THE HEALER

The Story of Francis Schlatter

Edited By
Norman Cleaveland

Sunstone Press
Santa Fe, New Mexico

ACKNOWLEDGEMENTS

The chapter entitled "The Healer Comes To Datil" is from NO LIFE FOR A LADY by Agnes M. Cleaveland. Copyright 1941 by Agnes Cleaveland. Copyright (c) renewed 1969 by Lorraine Lavender. Reprinted by permission of Houghton Mifflin Company.

The chapter entitled "The Copper Rod" is from CAMPFIRE AND TRAIL by Edgar L. Hewett published by the University Press and is used by permission of the University of New Mexico Press.

Printed in the United States of America

Library of Congress Cataloging in Publication Data:

Schlatter, Francis, 1856-1896?
  The healer : the story of Francis Schlatter / edited by Norman Cleaveland. — 1st ed.
    p.   cm.
  ISBN 0-86534-139-7 : $14.95
  1. Schlatter, Francis, 1856-1896? 2. Healers — United States -Biography. I. Cleaveland,
Norman. II. Title.
  RZ232.S3A3   1989
  615.8'52'092–dc20   89-19679
  (B)   CIP

Published in 1989 by SUNSTONE PRESS
              Post Office Box 2321
              Santa Fe, NM 87504-2321 / USA

CONTENTS

INTRODUCTION

In most generations there appears a person, usually a man, who has authenticated powers of healing and who acts, often, as a kind of messiah. This is a person who by his or her charisma and personal magnetism attracts a large following. In many cases such leaders protest this following and claim no personal glory or responsibilty for healing and other acts that are performed. Charlatan, miracle worker or deluded mystic ? Few contemporaries can ever decide and history itself is not sure. Such a person was Francis Schlatter but the opinion of the times was generally that he was an honest man, a genuine healer.

Schlatter, a German immigrant shoemaker and a devout Catholic, came to Denver in 1892. In 1893, presumably acting under divine guidance, he began a circuitous route through Kansas, Arkansas, Texas, Arizona, California, and New Mexico. Stories of his healing powers spread rapidly, especially among the inhabitants of the New Mexico Spanish villages who called him simply *El Sanador* (The Healer). It was reported that because of Schlatter the blind regained sight, the paralyzed could use their here-to-fore useless arms or legs, the crippled walk with ease, and the rheumatic move with unaccustomed agility.

In July, 1895, Schlatter moved to Albuquerque, New Mexico where he continued to perform his miraculous cures. While there were some who questioned his power and motives, it was universally acknowledged that he accepted no money for his deeds. It was also observed that if money was forced upon him, he would give it to the poor.

After staying in Albuquerque for about a month, Schlatter returned to Denver. Following a rest of a few weeks, he resumed his healing sessions. Thousands waited in line to touch or be touched by him. My interest in Schlatter starts here as this was when my grand-mother a devout Methodist, first met him. She was one of those who received his blessing.

Although thousands of people were anxious to see Schlatter, he suddenly disappeared from Denver. This was in November, 1895 and an immediate search was made to try and discover his whereabouts. It was reported that he had gone into hiding somewhere in New Mexico. In January of the next year he came to my grandmother's ranch in Datil, then in Socorro County, New Mexico. An account of that meeting and his subsequent stay there that culminated in the writing of the book, *The Life of the Harp in the Hand of the Harper* is found in the chapter, "The Healer' Comes to Datil" reprinted here from the book *No Life for a Lady* written by my mother, Agnes Morley Cleaveland. This is an eyewitness account of how my grandmother felt about Schlatter and why she felt compelled to write down and publish the manuscript he dictated to her while staying at the ranch.

When spring came in 1896 and after assuring Granny that he would return to the Datil mountains which would eventually provide the site for a new Jerusalem, Schlatter vanished from the ranch. One report said he had been near Silver City in April and then gone down into Mexico. Later it was reported that he had died in Chihuahua in 1896. The fact of his death was confirmed in 1906 by Dr. Edgar Lee Hewett, the noted archaeologist, while he was on an archaeological trip in Mexico. Dr. Hewett had known and talked with Schlatter when he was in Denver so perhaps it was only fitting that he should have been the one to verify what happened to Schlatter and to acquire the The Healer's rod. Hewett's account is in the chapter, "The Copper Rod", here reprinted from his book *Campfire and Trail*.

Despite the proof of Schlatter's death, various imposters continued to appear for at least the next twenty years. The important difference was that they usually accepted money for their services.

The mystery of who or what Francis Schlatter was can never really be solved. On several occasion he said that "The Father" had sent him on his healing mission. Certainly photographs of him show a saint-like figure with flowing hair and beard. The metal rod that he used for exercise was necessary, he claimed, to maintain his power. In keeping with his character, he also explained that these instructions had come from "The Father".

Francis Schlatter was like a comet — he burst upon the scene, burned brightly for a short time and then was gone. However, his book lives on as do the accounts of those who knew him and experienced his help.

Norman Cleaveland
Santa Fe / 1989

Mary E. McPherson (center) and her two daughters: Ada McPherson Morley (left), Norman Cleaveland's grandmother; and Mary (Mamie) McPherson (right). This photograph was taken circa 1893 at the graduation of Mamie from Wellesley College.

PART 1

'THE HEALER'
Comes to Datil

Grandmother McPherson's simple formula for salvation —
'Republican-Methodist-Teetotaler' — had never seemed to her
divinely authorized. But that a right formula did somewhere exist,
Mother unquestionably believed, and with a fervor equal to Grandmother McPherson's own she sought it. The day came when at last
she believed she had found it.

In the summer of 1895, a golden-bearded, blue-eyed, six-foot-tall
Alsatian cobbler named Francis Schlatter appeared in Albuquerque. He had just walked from California across the Mojave Desert,
living on little but bread made from unleavened flour which he
baked himself, and almost no water. This walk is considered impossible, yet the fact that he made it is amply authenticated.

Arrived in Albuquerque, he announced that as a final act of
spiritual preparation for his life mission, 'the Father' had bade him
fast for forty days. This fast took place in the home of people we
knew, and, according to them and scores of others, including
newspaper reporters, was genuine. At its finish, one who was present recorded that he ate a substantial meal of 'fried chicken,
beefsteak, and fried eggs.' No ill effect followed.

His fame became of headline importance, but it was not until he
appeared in Denver later in the same summer that Mother saw him.
She was one of thousands who stood in line to receive his blessing,
one that was reputed to carry healing.

Lest the conclusion be jumped at that it was only the weakminded
who stood for hours waiting to touch the hand of this peasant cobbler with his little-understood powers, let me say that on the special
trains that were run into Denver to accommodate the throngs who
believed in him were many intelligent and well-to-do people. A
person who was at the end of the line which formed daily and

stretched out for many city blocks at 6 a.m. counted himself lucky to stand in Schlatter's presence by noon. As many as five thousand in a day passed before him. In good journalistic style the newspapers gave accounts of healing claimed and miracles performed. In the line three stations ahead of my mother, a crippled negro woman inched painfully forward, hour after hour. Arrived at last where Schlatter stood in the gateway of the yard to a modest home, where he was being harbored, the negro woman stretched forth her hands to grasp those of the man before her. An instant later she threw her arms in the air and shouted, 'Praise Gawd, he done healed me, and he done give me back my dollar!'

Yes, he gave back all money proffered. That was never disputed. He took no pay.

Day after day he received the lame, the halt, and the blind, the rich and the poor, the educated and the ignorant. I refer you to the Denver daily press of the period, to the press of the whole United States, for details, and for claims of cures.

It was a reporter's paradise.

Then Schlatter disappeared, leaving behind him thousands of disappointed people. It was a disappearance that seemed miraculous, for he vanished on a big white horse. For weeks the boys of the press vied with one another in efforts to find him — solely for his news value. He was reported seen here, there, everywhere, only to have every clue fail. From the newsgatherers' standpoint it was exasperating and the determination to find him grew apace. The hunt assumed incredible proportions. Every white horse within a radius of several hundred miles was held suspect, but none of them was Schlatter's horse, Butte.

Then one winter night, seven weeks after he had seemingly vanished from the earth, a man who was doing some temporary work for Mother in Datil came to where she sat before an open fire reading, with the startling report: 'There's a man lying beside the barn and he had the gall to put his horse in the haystack corral. It's a great big white horse that'll sure make a hole in that stack by morning. I told the man to come over to the house or he'd freeze to death and he answered that he must be invited. He's *poco loco*, I guess, but he'll sure freeze if he stays where he is.'

A few moments later, Mother met the stranger with the cry, 'Francis Schlatter!' He nodded gravely. 'The Father has directed me to a safe retreat. I must restore my spiritual powers in seclusion and prayer.'

He had ridden the seven hundred miles between Denver and Datil in midwinter, much of the way in desolate rugged country, the last stretch across forbidding Putney Mesa, where snow lay over a foot deep. Yet Butte had arrived in exceedingly good condition.

For almost three months, Schlatter remained in an upstairs room, venturing out only when the coast was unmistakably clear. Two occupations engrossed him during this time: he dictated to my mother a manuscript of considerable length, which she later published under the title he gave to it, *The Life of the Harp in the Hand of the Harper*. The rest of the time he spent in swinging a bronze club very like a forty-pound baseball bat, as a drum major might swing a baton. It was a feat requiring prodigious strength, but he did it tirelessly. He said that it was a practice imposed upon him by 'the Father' and he must obey or lose his power.

Mother read him the newspaper accounts of the search still being made for him, to all of which he replied, 'When the time has come for me to reveal myself, the Father will tell me.'

Finally, one day a Mexican woman who came to do the washing noticed an extraordinarily large flat-heeled footprint in the yard, not at all the sort of imprint made by a spike-heeled cowboy boot. She suspected rightly whose it was — not surprising, with the big white horse still in the barnyard.

Immediately Mexicans from Quemado, from Mangas, from outlying ranches, began coming on flimsy pretexts, camping in the dooryard, and Mother was hard put to it not to lie outright. At last, Schlatter said to her, 'I must go.'

He saddled Butte, tied the brass rod to his saddle, and mounted. Then turning to Mother he said: 'Walk with me. I have things to tell you.'

She walked by his side for three miles, and by herself in a sort of rapt ecstasy the three miles' return trip. She believed! He said:

'You will have what will seem to be certain evidence of my death brought to you. The world will laugh at you for rejecting — but reject it! I shall not be dead. I will return to Datil. The Father has told me that Datil is the place He has selected for New Jerusalem. Wait for me.' Then he bade her go home.

Again he vanished, and for a decade impostors in unbroken succession appeared throughout the country claiming to be the original Schlatter, but all differing from him in the detail of returning any money proffered. A Los Angeles court sent one false Schlatter to jail, and all others were discredited. Meanwhile Mother waited with unfaltering faith. Nothing mattered any more. Schlatter would return and the world would be freed from its shackles.

My own part in the story was slight, but, slight as it was, baffling. As I have said, I did not go back to college that fall because I felt that one of us should remain with Mother. Her search for the Formular was engrossing her more and more. She spent longer hours in letter-writing and shorter ones on material concerns.

But since little ranch work goes on in midwinter I had decided in January that I could go to Stanford. I left her to her letters — letters to most of the leaders of thought of that era in this country, and not a few in foreign lands — and entered upon another bout of my battle to get an education. I had been gone only a day or two when Schlatter appeared at our house.

As usual, I returned to Datil for the summer vacation. As I approached the house riding with Mother in the buggy in which she had come to Magdalena to meet me, I gasped in surprise: 'WHAT is that?'

A design stood out boldly on the front of the west wing of the house, a design that I can best describe as a bent cross, the upright curving counter clockwise so the crossbar curved slightly upward. It was about ten feet high and it appeared to have been painted on the logs with whitewash.

'I thought I would let you see it first,' Mother said, uneasily, I felt. 'Perhaps it may help you to form a right judgment.'

'But what is it? Who put it there?'

'Nobody knows how it got there,' Mother told me. 'It appeared when Schlatter left.'

I hesitate to repeat the surmises that we all indulged in but stick strictly to facts. No tracks showed where someone had brought a ladder; there was no ladder on our place, nor whitewash. Our dog had not barked in the night.

'What do you think it means?' I asked, and it was my turn to feel uneasy, dreading what her explanation might suggest.

'Well' — Mother seemed to be choosing her words carefully — 'the upper part is a sort of map of the pilgrimages which the Healer' — she spoke the title reverently — 'has already taken: north and south from Cheyenne to El Paso, east to Datil; I interpret it as meaning that he will finish the cross by going deep into Old Mexico. I interpret it as meaning that until the cross is completed by his journeyings I must wait for him.'

I looked at her with troubled eyes.

It was in Old Mexico that, ten years later, the newspapers thought they had discovered him. A clipping was handed to my mother which told that under a tree in Chihuahua had been found a man's skeleton, a peculiar metal rod, a weather-faded Bible with the name Francis Schlatter on the fly-leaf.

'He told me to expect this,' Mother said quietly. 'He is not dead.

He will return.'

Thereafter we walked in the presence of one who was with us but not of us. The home life went on around her but she was no longer interested in it. She was now sure that a short-cut into the Eternal City was to be opened through the tortuous mountains of human struggle.

Agnes Morley Cleaveland (circa 1900)

The Morley ranch house, known as the "White House", in Datil, New Mexico.

PART 2

THE
LIFE OF THE HARP

IN THE HAND OF
THE HARPER

By FRANCIS SCHLATTER

Complied and Published in Obedience to his Commands, by his
Hostess, at present in Denver, Colorado.
P.O. Box 398.

1896

DENVER, COLORADO
THE SMITH-BROOKS PRINTING COMPANY
1897

PREFACE.

In compiling this book it has not been the intention to include an exhaustive biography of Francis Schlatter or a detailed account of the extent and results of his work as a healer. The latter, at least, is too well known as a matter of contemporaneous history to require exploitation here. The sole intention has been to give to the world the writings and teachings left by the Healer for the world — to give them as nearly as possible in his own quaint language, and to accord them the prominence which rightfully appertains to them, both by reason of the Healer's habitual taciturnity and because they appear here for the first time. In addition to those writings and teachings only enough other matter has been inserted to afford some continuity between the Healer's own description of his two years' time of tribulation and the precepts subsequently dictated by him in the seclusion of the mountain ranch. The interpolation consist of the chapters on "The Fast in Albuquerque" and "The Healer in Denver." The former is written by "Fitz Mac" of Denver and is reprinted from a Chicago publication by special permission. The latter was written for this work by Mr. Joseph Wolff of Boulder, Colorado. To both of those gentlemen grateful acknowledgments are due for the favors named, as well as to Mrs. Grace L. Brown, Mrs. Lucien Scott, Mr. and Mrs. Charles N. Whitman and Mrs. Hullings of Denver, to Mr. and Mrs. Wolff of Boulder, to Mr. Victor Slayton, recently of Grand Rapids, Michigan, who gave time and attention to this volume, and to others whose many courtesies have made the continuance of the Healer's work possible to

HIS HOSTESS

INTRODUCTION.

Secular history has no parallel to this voluntary, yet involuntary pain. We search, therefore, for like Spiritual realities in Holy Writ of the various Bibles of humanity.

The soul had gone on a quest for God — had sought and found — before this Spiritual work was made manifest to men.

From youth up he had feared God and kept His commandments. Kind-hearted, considerate and generous to the extreme, it seems the Unseen Powers chose this gentle, trusting, loving nature to be the willing instrument to teach humanity. He consecrated the energies of his life in obedience to the Voice of this Unseen Intelligence.

The active Love Principle took possession of Francis Schlatter in 1892, in New York State, being in his 37th year, while there working patiently and hopefully. Meantime he was a constant reader and thinker, endeavoring to see for the race a way out of appalling conditions. In imagination we can see him, after the stifling stress of a wearing workday, pondering the mighty problems of life; studying, as he burned the midnight oil, our language unaided and alone. Reading of the Christ method of healing, that thought resulted in a sweeping self-interrogation — "Others heal, why may I not?" The then unrecognized, though Guiding Hand, had led him to Denver in the ninth month of that same year.

Yes, the soul had gone on a quest, being prepared, not only by virtue of his previous life, but by vision in his Downing avenue work shop, where he resisted and dreaded for four months the ardent yet abstruse admonition of the Father's Voice, which said:

"Follow me. Come out into a world of woe alone, and I will make you the greatest Healer since Jesus and give you a New Name."

In the sixth month after his arrival in that psychic center, Denver, he had a remarkable vision of the trinity, which he ever interpreted as the conception of his spiritual life and power, the Inception of marvelous soul-growth and progress.

About 3 o'clock, March 25th, 1893, though not in a trance, dream or other abnormal condition, but as we may say, by the inner eye, he saw the Father, Son and Spirit personified. He beheld the Father seated, holding a Book in the left hand — The Book of Life. Jesus was upon His right. On the left the Spirit, the similitude of Jesus. Whereupon Jesus arose, walked to him and handed him the Lily. From that hour he heard audibly the Father's Voice, as Joan of Arc heard her "beautiful voices" years before she left her humble home in Domremy. Voice and Vision are as deep and profound realities to the one as they were to the other.

The hidden struggle that took place in the secret recesses of this soul, we may never know. Yet we find the Chosen One could not start immediately. He waited, shrinking in contemplation of the pain; he hesitated, fully conscious of the significance to both the redeemer and the redeemed; he lingered, realizing the method and meaning, questioning the fathomless deeps of spirituality as no one else could. Finally, resting in and trusting the Universal First Cause, he became strong enough; being fully assured and satisfied, the soul surgings having ceased, he turned for the last time the key of the work-shop door, and walked away from Denver.

From birth he had been preparing for this strange and mystic mission; and who may say for how many centuries or aeons before the present physical expression?

This humble Alsatian was obedient ever to the Voice. Yet in that long and lonely march, as he crossed and recrossed the vast stretches, bare-headed and barefooted, in interminable and unnamable agony, he often cried in anguish:

"Father, have mercy!"

"No mercy for you. Follow me and I will do the rest," was the invariable response of the Invincible and Inscrutable Power, leading and guiding him on his perilous journey.

The following brief record is only an epitomized narration of his 730 awful days of superhuman endurance, traversing eight western states and territories in scorching heat of deserts and bitter cold of mountains, always hungry, naked or imprisoned.

If faith be dead to-day, as the many affirm, here was One willing to suffer, listening to and believing in the promises of Scripture, living the words so meaningless to the mass of mankind, "Though He slay me, yet will I trust Him." Here we behold One holding fast the Bible promises to those who have ears to hear; here the latest, highest phase of the religious devotee; here the rare beauty of steadfastness and unflinching following to the end.

We are awed to stillness in sympathetic contemplation! What a pathetic picture! What an unearthly contrast!

While the world was whirling in modern luxurious ease back and forth to that veritable Fairyland of art and beauty; while the reading, thinking, and serious were attending the First Congress of All Religious, this lone traveler of trust was lying in dirty ditches beside railroad tracks, eating betimes what was hurled by servants of the rich from Pullman cars, sleeping unprotected in Kansas corn fields, tortured both mentally and physically, and yet, when thus dealt with, happy and hopeful he went his way, a Spiritual Tramp, knowing he would ultimately help poor and downtrodden humanity by the spiritual union with the Father. However, sometimes he murmured, when cold and half starved:

"Father, you give me too much to die, but not enough to live!" To this came the severe reply:

"When I want you to have food you will have it. Follow me!"

To us how cold and cruel seem the commands, yet *he knew* it to be the Voice of Our Father Who art in Heaven, whose very name is hallowed.

Where another of so mighty faith? Sublimely alone this walker! A constant struggle, yet with only *one purpose* — the prospective establishment of the Kingdom of God, here and now! With but one motive — immeasurable Love of Humanity! He asked no questions as to how or when, only obeying and going to the end.

The closing years of this century and cycle seem both blessed and privileged by the presence of this Great Soul on our planet, whose every breath is the inbreathing of the Lord's Prayer, whose every thought only of the time when Father will bring him back to aid in the work of social reconstruction; to hearken to the Father in his Judgment Day and help to establish Justice.

But how are we to reconcile the apparently severe tyranny of this Unseen Intelligence with our preconceived notions of a loving God? How explain the seeming cruelty of the Father's commands to this humble, willing, obedient soul? Only by accepting the Healer's own words to illumine our darkness and doubt:

"It all has an object. Father is tired of talk. Why do they not live their words? He wants deeds, not words. He has promised for ages to establish the Kingdom. Did not Jesus say, 'The meek shall inherit the earth?' Who inherits the earth to-day? Could Father make false promises? Why say and not do?"

Therefore, with him, who seems to know the Unknowable, who has attained the summit of faith, who is one with the Father, let us look beyond the Pain to the Infinite Eternal Purpose.

HIS HOSTESS.

Hermosillo Ranch,
    Datil, New Mexico.
October, 1896.

Francis Schlatter in 1895.

CHAPTER I.

THE TWO YEARS' PILGRIMAGE.

The first night's experience was after a thirty-four-mile walk from Denver on the Union Pacific towards Cheyenne, July 20th, 1893. It was down in a deep hollow or pond, where were many trees. At first I had a lot of mosquitoes. For hours they were a certain distance from me, but none came to me; but all at once all came and nearly devoured me.

The next night I slept in a straw heap; the third night in a barn. When, in the morning, I was thrown by Satan, I got up at 2 o'clock and just said, "I will not tramp." Then of course Father took away the guidance because of such rebellion. That lasted for three hours, for I asked as usual, but no response. So I said, "If you are angry, I must be too. I will tramp no more." But I had to come back. I had started to return to Denver and I kept going, but Father did not mind so long as I was willing to go.

The fourth day I met many of the unemployed. I was near a water tank with a good many of them. Some were very depressed. I was out of my sphere and went about Father's business, but by the remarks and their looks, as well as questions they asked, I knew they were planning something. In those days of course I was well dressed and had a watch. I told them I would walk all night and they answered, "We will overtake you because we will take the express." But instead of walking Father told me to lie down, and He found me a place in which to sleep, a few hundred yards from the railroad.

On the fifth I walked all day, but on wagon roads, until night came. I hardly could see. Before I knew, I was in a cactus bed, and again all night the mosquitoes were terrible, and the next morning I came back to Denver. But the feet were blistered and greatly swollen, so I thought to make me a pair of sandals. But I asked first if I could have them, and He told me I could. So I bought a pair of soles and made them. I asked Father if He would let me buy some half-soles, also take a few tools, enough to repair shoes along the road so I would have something to live on. He told me I could buy the leather. The next day I started in the afternoon from Downing avenue, came to Colfax, then took the electric road through Fairview. I crossed a river, then kept going till Father told me to stop. I went into a fenced lot far away from the road, when in about half an hour it began to rain; so I asked if I could not go to a house about a mile north. The answer was "Yes." So hurrying I went, but I was wet before I got there, and it was empty. What a horrible storm that night! I stayed the following day and night, during another horrible storm, without food or water. The next day I started, but my pack got so heavy it seemed it weighed a hundred pounds more than when I started. Again I came to an empty house, and there was a windmill near the road, and I fell exhausted, because Father had an object, and that was to throw away that leather, those nails, pincers, hammer and the iron last. But I said:

"Father, how will I live? I have only $3.75 in money. How can I undertake such a trip without money?

The answer came back:

"I will take care of you."

Of course I know He can take care of me if He wants to, and I never ask how. So I asked:

"You want me to throw all of this away?"

"Yes," He said. So I laid it in the house. I thought it would be useful to somebody. It is under cover, somebody will find it and make use of it. Then I started onward with my sandals on my feet.

That night it rained again. In fact it rained every day and night. In the morning about 2 o'clock I was so wet and so cold, when all at once a shooting pain went through my left breast. I knew that pain, it was pleurisy. So I said:

"Well, I'm in a nice fix now! Out here on the prairie, sick and cold — what shall I do?"

"Yes, you have pleurisy, but you will not have it long." In about five minutes the pain was all gone and I have felt no more of it since.

I went on my journey, but my feet troubled me terribly, and while sitting and resting a fellow came along and asked for ten cents. I said, "I can not give it to you because Father does not want me to." He looked and said, "You have a good outfit," then walked on a little way, turned and came back, asking the same thing. But he went away like a lamb, to return again, but then left me.

It rained all the afternoon and the night was cold and wet. The following day was Sunday, and I was resting. Toward 5 o'clock a storm was coming from East, West, North and South, and as it rained I wanted to go back to those houses, but I had to go ahead, and it poured till 12 o'clock at night. The darkness and lightning were appalling, and I was so wet, cold, tired and hungry. I sat down on a railroad tie, when the express passed. I said to Father, "Those who are in there are happier than I." But the answer was, "No, you are happier than they." So I started and kept walking till daylight. I passed Limon, then I took the Rock Island and kept on going.

Passed the night in a ditch along the railroad near Aden. Next morning went to a section house east of Aden and asked to buy a loaf of bread. She wanted to give me butter, meat and coffee, but I told her that I could not eat those things. I could only eat bread and drink water every other day, or sometimes every two days, and she wanted to know why. I told her that I had to walk, fast, sleep out of doors, and be alone; then Father would make me a great healer. When I had eaten I wanted to pay her, but she would not have anything. I started off again on my journey, walking all day, and at night the wind was blowing cold, so I lay in a deep ditch. I was quite comfortable when, at 11, it began to rain again and rained all night, so I walked all night. Towards morning I came to a station and went in to warm, when I came to the conclusion that that would not do. I said to Father, "If you only would let me buy six yards of unbleached muslin, at least I would not get wet nights." Father said I could have it, so I bought the stuff and made a small tent. But from that day it did not rain where I was save once, while I had the tent.

When I went out of the station to buy that stuff the section men started to work, and they saw me walking in sandals, and the section boss said, "Look! here is a fellow that looks like an apostle!" but I kept on my journey. While walking along the track the section men went over to inspect it, and they passed me again. Father afterwards told me to wait for hours at the same place. I wanted to go on but I could not. I had to stay there until Father told me to go ahead. At last word came and I went on. Soon from afar off I saw the section gang at work, and when I drew near the boss left his men and came to see me. He asked questions and I told him, and he believed. Then he told me that his wife was very sick, but that she was in New York state. I told him, "That makes no difference if they only believe." As it was toward evening he asked me to go with him on the hand car to the section house. It was a day in which I could eat, so I ate biscuit and drank water. They wanted me to drink coffee and eat pie, but I was forbidden to eat those things and I had to obey. The next morning I left on my journey onward, leaving eastern Colorado and entering western Kansas.

I met one day two little boys and they told me their father had sowed much wheat and corn, but all was burned out. "So we are herding horses," said he, "that we may have some bread to eat. Take care of the farm with my mother, and father has gone away to Wyoming to find something to do but we got a letter that he had tried in every way but could find no work. Somebody offered him some cattle to herd, so we will have some bread to eat during the winter, for he brings them here." I talked with them about two hours and then had to go on.

I said to Father, "What a horrible world! Here is a family; they want to do, but everything is against them. Those children said they would be thankful if they only had bread to eat. Look at that boy. In him the spirit was right. I suppose you gave me another lesson of the suffering of the world. I wish I could do something for those two little boys!"

Father answered, "You have done already what no human can do. I will give them wisdom, foresight and contentment for the present; and for the future, they will see and understand, when the time comes, your great work which you have to execute; but when my time comes, not your time. Then they will get their reward."

The days passed, walking, fasting, sleeping out of doors as onward I went, when I met another little boy. He saw me coming and waited. We sat down on a railroad tie and he told me that his family came from lower Texas, because some of them were sick. "But," said he, "we have had such a bad time since we are here. Almost every year the crops have burned up. This year we have not feed enough for our cattle, and we are soon going to leave for Texas again." Then he said suddenly, "Are you hungry?" If you are I will get you something to eat. I often give poor men something to eat."

"Yes, I am hungry, but I have yet a little money, and as long as I have, I want to pay for food. I would be very glad if I could buy a loaf of bread."

"I will ask mother if she can spare a loaf." So I gave him a quarter and a tin pail to bring me some water, and off he went like a shot.

On that morning when I started to walk I was so cold I wished I might get some coffee, but my wishes are nothing. "If you do not want me to have I can not have." Then the boy came back with the loaf of bread and the pail of water, and I began to eat because I was very hungry, when the boy said suddenly,

"Would you like some coffee?" Mother has some. It will not cost you anything," and before I could speak the boy was gone. I asked Father if I could drink it and He told me, "Yes." No one can understand how happy I was, for that was only the second time I had had anything warm since I left Denver.

On I came to Goodland, hungry and thirsty looking for a baker. I bought a loaf of bread. He said, "Did you come from the depot?" I said "Yes." He said, "Ten cents." I paid him and asked for water. Then he asked if I was traveling on the cars, and I said, "No, I have to walk." He gave me back five cents saying, "We sell to the traveling people at one price and to the poor at another."

When I came back to the railroad a switchman said to wait a little while and I could take that train just pulling out. I told him that I could not ride on trains, that I had to walk, and onward I went. But it was nothing but fasting and walking until I came to Colby. It was west of there I had to wait till Father gave the word to move. The section boss came up to say, "Hello, are you alive under there?" I had tied one end of my little sheet of cotton to a telegraph pole, at the other end I placed a broomstick, then a rope across, that it could not fall in, and on either side were four pegs. Of course I had to crawl under. From there I answered, "I am here."

"Are you not afraid of rattlesnakes? The country is full of them!" said he.

"I? No. I have no need to be afraid of either man or beast."

Then he asked me many questions. I told him what my mission was and he believed. So I went on again. In the afternoon, being on the east end of his section, we had another talk, and while we were talking the express train passed. The water barrel was standing upon the hand car out of the way, because the hand cear never moved, neither did the barrel — but the cover of it was thrown fifteen feet away, although it was screwed on. After this I went on my way again.

Passed Phillipsburg and, on the 21st of August came to Pendleton. I had my last ten cents, with which I bought a loaf of bread. I had picked up a few apples and, taking the pail of water went into an empty place near the station. It was very cold and raining. While sitting eating and drinking the water, the owner of the house came with a painter to show and make estimates. When they stepped in one can have no idea how I felt, because I was on another man's property. He showed himself to be a good man. He did not say anything but went on with his business, and I kept on until I had finished; then went about half a mile along the railroad to sleep. But it rained the bigger part of the night, so I walked. And the next day when the sun shone warm, Father told me to sleep.

Toward evening I began to feel ill, bad; and so it was all that night and for two days. The third day I went a little farther, but He gave me no strength. I could hardly stand on my feet. A section man gave me a little bread, and I went a little farther. In the night I came around a curve. There were some old ties and I bethought me that it was better to lie on them than on the ground. I was terribly weak and the lightning and thunder were frightful, though not much rainfall. The next day was pleasant, but Father told me to stay. A farm house was just opposite, but they were very good people. The man saw me and came over to me and asked questions. I told him my mission, then asked for water. He said I could have water, and also offered bread and butter. But before taking I asked if I could, and Father said "Yes."

The third day, on a Monday, a section boss told me, "Move on or I will put you where they will take care of you." I answered him, "I will go." Went to the farm house and got some more water. The wife gave me some bread and butter. The man asked me if I was going away, and I told him I had been ordered away by the section boss. I returned to the railroad to eat the bread, when a young fellow came along and asked which way I was going.

"East. I have been ordered away, and they threatened to put me in the dry."

"I wish they would put me in the dry." said he, "for I've hunted long for work and can not find any."

So I went east and he went west, but being very weak I went only seven miles. I came to a curve and quite a deep cut. There was a big pile of dirt on the south side. I examined it and thought it a good place, because nobody could see me from the railroad. I asked Father and He told me to stay there three days and nights without food or water. I obeyed. Then left that place and went a little farther and sighted a farm house about half a mile from the railroad. I went over to get some water. I met the man and we soon drifted in our talk on to the situation of the whole country.

I returned to the road and stayed there that night, and the next day went on, though very weak, till it was quite dark. I was nearing Formosa, so I put up the little tent and upset a part of the little water I had. There I stayed three days and nights before anybody knew. On a Sunday I lay under my little canvas. It was terribly hot, about the 3rd of September. I tried to get up but raised myself a little too fast and fell down. Then I crawled again under the canvas and said to Father:

"You saw what happened just now. You want me to fast yet till next Thursday. But how can I fast till that time, for I can't stand on my feet? Now, here I am, out on the prairie, without money, and even if I had money you would not let me get anything."

Then the Father said, "Do not worry. When I want you to have water you will have water."

"But now shall I get it?"

"Someone will bring it to you," said He, "and when I want you to eat you will have food."

"Cold or warm?" I asked.

"Cold, and on next Thursday; but you will have the patience."

So I calmed down and had a good night's sleep, but the next day was very hot and I suffered from thirst. But toward evening a man passed and came to see who was under the canvas. Shortly he sent me water by his children. They brought me more water next morning; and by noon a young man brought me lunch. But it lay there, hungry and weak as I was. Then came along the commissioner of the poor, because the man who had sent me the water got scared and reported I was dying. But I told him all. Then he asked me to go with him, and promised to care for me. But I told him no one could induce me to eat while I had to fast. Then he said, "There is no danger of that man dying. He looks all right, but I shall see you again," and off he went.

That afternoon came Mr. Dwyer, of the township of Formosa, with his two daughters and a young man. He questioned me. I told him all. He replied that he came to see me because it was a novelty to see a man traveling in that way in our days. Then we had a long talk. On leaving he offered me a box of crackers.

Two officers of the law came from Formosa with intentions to arrest me, but when I told them I heal, and that I have another Spiritual work to do which will be greater than that of Moses when he took the Children of Israel out of Egypt, they said, "We had better leave you alone" and went off quietly. When they had gone I asked Father if I could eat.

"O! Father, I wish you would give me one day less! I pray, let me eat. I am so hungry!" I begged and prayed to eat the food beside me, when suffering from hunger, and at last He told me that I could. It such a surprise to me that I asked twice before I could touch the food. But when I was sure, I began and did eat.

The next day Charley Gumm took me to his place because his brother's little girl had hip disease. I stayed there, camping out of doors nights, till Sunday, when wagon load upon wagon load of people came to see "The crazy man," as they liked to call me. The same afternoon the owner of the farm told the man I was staying with that I would have to go on or he too would have to leave. I told

Mr. Gumm that I did not want him to have trouble. I left the next day at 7 o'clock going onward. The following day I was on the Santa Fe.

I came to a cross-roads and Father told me to sit down. I sat there, waiting quietly, when after a while a young boy came along and asked questions. I told him, and then he went to the postoffice, and the first thing I knew there came the Kackley Courier editor. He asked me if I would not come to the office, as the proprietor wanted to speak with me. I asked Father and was told to go. I stayed with him that afternoon and he took me home to supper, and they asked questions. I told him all my experiences since I left Denver, and Mr. Ziegler said it was a strange life. At 10 o'clock at night Father told me to go, and He took me to the westward. I slept in a cornfield. A little farther along the road I stayed three days, with two ears of raw corn that I picked daily. Then I had to go.

I came to a peach orchard. I stayed there three days, but all I could eat was one ear of raw corn. Then I had to go.

I went along the road four days without food when, on the fourth day, Father stopped me at a small house and well. A young man brought me bread and butter and some milk; then told me the place had gone into other hands. And the one who was going to take possession said he was going to have me arrested if I did not leave. So I told the young man I was going on and on.

The next day I went a little further and Father stopped me near a hedge. The nights were cold and I stayed there three days, with three slices of bread. At last he told me to go on and I went over to a farm house to the windmill to get a drink. I had no water for three days. The man came along and told me the windmill was broken, but I came to the house. He asked questions and I told him. I had bread, butter, cake and coffee, and on I went, walking late into the night. The wind was blowing cold from the east, and I came to a hedge, and He said to go inside the hedge and follow on. Then He told me to lie down. On Sunday night two men on horseback came along about 10 o'clock, asking questions, and I told them I heal. They answered, "If you heal why do you not go into houses?" I said, "I can't go to them but they have to come to me." Then they asked me if I would preach. I said, "No."

"Are you not afraid somebody will hurt you?"

"Nobody can hurt me," I answered, and one remarked, "Only send him a chunk of beef and a shock of whiskey and he will be all right," and they moved off.

The next day a man came along and asked me to go with him and eat, saying, "Father does not want you to fast; you are mistaken."

then my spirit began to rise and I told him I knew what I had to do. There I had to stay three days and night without food or drink. When, at 11 o'clock at night, Father woke me up and told me to leave that place, I had to walk all night and all next day, and about 4 o'clock I went through Beloi. Nearly five miles east I came to a straw heap, in the middle of which was a deep hole. Father told me I must stay there three days and nights. All I was permitted to eat during that long walk was three ears of raw corn—one each day—but could have no water.

The third day was cloudy and threatened rain all day, more and more toward evening. About 5 o'clock He told me, "Go on and tonight you will be under a roof." I passed many farm houses when at last I came to a place where the house stood back from the road with an orchard in front of it. Father told me to go in and ask for shelter. By this time it was pouring rain, and the man came out and I asked for shelter. He invited me in and they were just through supper. I had some supper and dried myself. It was something new to dry myself near a stove, for I had always had to dry my clothes on me when wet. It poured at night. The next morning they invited me to breakfast. Now, if there is anything I like, it is pancakes. Those pancakes — they looked so good. But Father said, "You can not have breakfast," and that settled the cakes and molasses.

After a while the sun began to shine; it dried the roads up and I went on my journey. Walked all day, and the day following had some raw corn. I had to stop to eat this uncooked corn because, from mastication, my mouth became raw, or in other words, the skin of the mouth was worn off from the long period of eating this dry, hard corn.

So next day I was terribly hungry and my mouth was too sore to eat raw corn. Then I said to Father, "You promised to take care of me. Now, I have no money and am hungry. How shall I get something to eat?"

Father said to me, "Go over to this farm house and ask them for something to eat and they will give it to you." I cried. "Is that the way you are going to take care of me?"

"Yes," said he, and I felt as if struck by lightning.

I said, "You want me to go and beg? I will go, but under other circumstances I never would," and then I went. The man came to the door and I asked:

"Can I get something to eat?" He turned around to his wife and asked if she had anything.

"Yes," she said, "but I'll have to go to the cellar for it." He told me to sit down, that it would be ready in a few minutes. The table was soon set and she called me. That was my first good meal. And I did eat. I remember the mashed potatoes, beans, gravy, milk and dessert. I speak of this meal, for I have been so hungry! Nobody knows. When through, I went again to the parlor. The man asked where I came from. I told him from Denver, and we naturally came upon the situation and talked awhile. He asked me if I needed a stamped envelope to write to the Denver office before I reached Hot Springs. I felt humiliated. He saw it and said, "I'll give you a stamped envelope," and so he did. By this circumstance they can remember to whom they gave that meal the first Saturday of October.

On a Sunday I came to Dan Driscoll's, twenty miles from Courtland. Father said, "You go in here and they will give you to eat, but do not speak about the healing, even if they ask questions. So I did just the way Father told me as to what to do and to say, and naturally the discussion fell upon the situation of the world and this land in particular. He was a good Populist, and I was on the same opinion while I was yet on Long Island and also when I left Denver. But by this time knew differently. I knew better, and knew nothing earthly could break the bonds of Hell but the Creator Himself, though I could not see how. But I was certain, He can do it. And He promised that He will, when His own time comes. Father has always told me, "All you have to do is to follow Me and I will do the rest;" and I am determined to go the end.

Mr. Driscoll invited me to stay, as it was Sunday, and rest so I would be in better shape for my trip to Hot Springs, also adding that he would rather have his job to cut wood for the winter than to walk to Hot Springs. I told him, "Father will provide," and he said, "So He will."

The second day after leaving I was sitting along the roadside on my blanket when a carriage with a bay team came along and the man stopped and asked me what I was doing. I told him I was tired and taking a rest. Again he asked where I came from. I told him, Denver.

"I know you boys from Denver have it very hard. I asked you all these questions because I am sheriff of this county," said he. "And where are you going?"

"To Hot Springs," was my answer.

"You have a terrible walk ahead of you. Have you any more hope?"

"More than ever," I said He smiled and off he went. But little he knew what I meant.

Walking, walking, I came to a big farm house and Father said,

"Go in here and they will hide themselves." Then he took me to another large farm house and they did the same thing; and when I came away He said, "Now, go get some ears of corn." Onward I went, walking very late. I came to a place on the right hand side. In going east there was a park. I came to a road and Father said, "Go in here," and I went. I came to a house but no answer. Then I went to the back part of the house. On opening the door I found it was empty. So I asked Father if I could sleep there. I inspected the house in the dark and said, "Can I sleep in this which was the front room." And He said, "Yes." So I spread my blanket and lay down. But after a while I felt something I never had felt before, and, had it been under any other circumstances, I would have got out of there! I would rather sleep in a cornfield. But it does not matter what is in here. Nothing can hurt me. The Father is protecting me. And I went to sleep. I slept, and I saw. Then I said, "I do not care to sleep in another place like it." I went off in the morning at daybreak, and after a while I came to a house and Father told me to go in and ask for something to eat; that they would give it to me. They were poor farmers. I went and received food. On my way again a man passed me with a team and carriage, and he asked me if I wanted to have a ride, and Father said that I could go. Of course he asked me where I came from and I told. Then he asked where I was going, and I said, "Hot Springs." Then naturally we came upon the situation of this country, finance and all. When we reached Clay Center he put his carriage in livery stable, and I walked on, when he called me back and gave me twenty-five cents and said, "Go and have a dinner in some restaurant." But Father told me, "You keep the money. You will need it further on. I will get you a dinner." Then he took me through Clay Center, then south, then east. About five miles from the city there was a creek and a wooded thicket of only a few hundred yards. When I came to the other side I saw a road, on each side of which were rows of trees and a house at the end. Father said, "It is here you will have dinner." After knocking, the man came and I asked if I could have something to eat. He gave me a look and almost instantly he said, "Walk in." Then Father said, "You see they have the faith. They not only pray, but they execute their prayers in their daily life by their works; and this household does My will."

In time dinner was ready and I ate with them at the family table; and the man of the house never asked me one question. They feed many unfortunates, but to remember this: The day I ate with them they entertained friends who came from the fair in Chicago, an elderly man and a girl about twenty years of age.

On I went, day after day, through the wild-cat road. I came to the river and along there was snubbed by many, and I came to Manhattan. Went over the bridge and came to St. Mary's, then Topeka. The twenty-five cents then came handy. I was hungry and Father said, "You buy ten cents' worth of bread and ten cents' worth of cheese." I ate the bread and cheese on a street corner, sitting on my pack. It was dark, and when I had finished eating I went to a house and asked for a drink of water. Then I went on and came to a railroad bridge, and Father said, "You go down that bank and under that you can sleep." So down I go. It was so dark that I could see hardly anything, and I came along to bushes and weeds but at last found a little clear spot. Spreading my blankets I lay down and had a good sleep. In the morning, when Father told me, I got up and ate the rest of my bread and cheese. Then the men who work in the shops went over the bridge, and they were joking about me to one another, and they said, no doubt, judging by their action, "There is another bum."

When through with the bread and cheese rolled my blanket and my little canvas and up the bank I climbed, over that bridge and right through those railroad shops. Oh! I was happy when I was through! Out again among the flowers, and the birds gave me their sweet melody. Then again was I among my friends. But on, going through very rough roads to Lawrence. When I came to the bridge I turned and went to Olathe.

The north wind was blowing very cold. For thirty-six hours I had not tasted food, and it was a rebuke, revile; and Father took me to another place. I met an old man whose hair was white. He was in good circumstances, too, and I ask him if he would give me something to eat, the Father told me he prayed much. And he straightened up and he said, "Look at me! I am an old man, and you are a young man, and you ask me for something to eat."

I said to him, "If I ask you for something to eat 'tis because I am hungry," and I walked away.

But Father provided for me that night.

I was on the Fort Scott & Kansas railroad, and on I walked day after day. On a Sunday Father brought me to a large estate along the railroad, and He said, "You go in here and ask them for something to eat." I went and met the lady and her husband and I asked for something to eat. She answered, "The cook and all are in church, but wait a minute and I will see if I can find anything."

During that period her husband asked me where I came from and what I was doing. Father said, "Shoemaking," and I said, Shoemaking." The reason for that was, if I said, "I heal," they would not believe and would get prejudiced. They might also have said hard words and thereby have laid a curse upon themselves, and He did not want them to do that, because they feed many a hungry one. They not only pray, but they do His words, which is the fulfillment of their prayers. The lady gave me bread and jelly.

I thanked her and walked away into the orchard and went on my journey. That night I passed Paola and Father took me to the right and left in the country roads, when on a Sunday morning I came to a house. Father said, "You go in here." I went. The door was open. And there I saw the grandmother blind and the grandson blind also. That boy, though blind, when I spoke, walked forward and stood still in front of me, and his attitude meant, "Here he is."

When his mother came I asked her for some thing to eat, and her answer was, "I have nothing cooked," and yet that boy in front of me! But I had to go, and when alone with the birds and flowers I could not refrain from crying. Father took me to that place to lift an old curse which He had put upon that family because they had mistreated true and faithful people. Then He took me there to give them a chance, but they threw it away, and instead of Father lifting the old curse He laid a new curse upon them, because they serve Him only with their lips.

On and on I went, and Father provided for me. I came to the Indian Territory, weary and tired and I said, "You can give me rest if you only want to." And that same evening I was in a house and stayed for a week. Their name was Larkin. There I left my little canvas. Then I walked on, wading the big river, and onward I went through the woods; and Father took me to Indians as well as white people — back, forward, around and about. Finally on a Sunday afternoon a wild sow tried to attack me, but about five yards from me she stopped. She went back from me a little way and came for me again, but stopped in the same place went away again and came the third time, only to stop as before; all of which was done quicker than I can write it. I walked on and there was the sow yet standing, looking after me, though I had walked three hundred yards.

In three miles I came to a house of Americans. They kept a grocery store. I felt bad. The stomach was out of order. I suffered for five or six hours, then I went and asked, the lady cooked for me. I had my meal and thanked them for it. I was then about six miles of Tahlequah. I passed the town in the dark and kept going into the prairie. From afar off I saw a light. It was like a beacon. I came to it and found a church. Father said, "Go in." So I laid my pack outside and went in the church. But everybody looked at me. When the service was over I went out, took up my pack, and went on. At last I came to a house and Father said, "Go in here and ask for shelter." I did wish they would give me shelter. I felt bad; the frost had come down already. When I came to the door I knocked, and I heard them praying their family prayers. Somebody came to the door and I asked for shelter only, but they said they had no room, and they said there was a cabin across the prairie and only a lone man lived there. So I started, but afterward had to sleep on the prairie. It was much colder than in the woods, and there was a very heavy frost. I was terribly cold and sick all day and night. Next morning I made the wish that I could only have some pancakes and molasses, and then Father said. "You shall have it."

In passing through the woods I found a road and Father told me to follow that; it would take me to a house. And sure enough, I found a house went in and got the breakfast I had wished for and they received me very well. When two miles from there my right foot began to swell, and I took the shoe off. Father said, "You had better throw those shoes away. You can never put them on again."

"Yes, but it is cold," I answered.

Father said, "Jesus walked barefooted and bareheaded. You can walk also."

"But," said I, "Jesus was in a warm climate and I am in a cold one."

"That makes no difference. I want you to walk barefooted and bareheaded."

So I said, "Well, if you want it I will do it." I threw the shoes away, as well as the hat. I walked on in the cold, but a happiness came over me I had never known before, and I began to sing hymns.

That foot hurt awfully and kept on swelling and toward 1 o'clock in the afternoon it was so swollen you could not see the ankle joint. I could walk no longer. I had to lie down. And the nearest house behind me was three miles away. Then I lay in the woods and could not move, and I lay there the rest of the day. In the night the pain were so intense that I was moaning, when an owl screeched right in the oak tree which I lay under. Such horrible screeches I never heard. So I kept still and moaned, not aloud, but bore it silently. When daylight came I was glad. I lay there all day and could not move, but late in the afternoon a half-breed Indian farmer and his wife, who was an American and had been raised in the Territory, came along. He stopped his wagon and asked me questions. I showed him my foot. He asked me how long I had been there. I told.

"And you have had nothing to eat or drink all that time? I never saw a man so cheerful under such suffering. But I am sorry I am going away from home. It is eighteen miles to the house in Tahlequah, but if you are here tomorrow I will take you to our home." And he went on his journey.

That night there was a severe thunder storm, and it rained all night very hard. I was drenched through all night, and that foot! I could not move the least. I had to lie and take it. About 10 o'clock the next morning the sun began to shine. It was quite warm, when three men on horseback came from Tahlequah. They asked me, and I showed them my foot. Then they wanted to know how long I had been there, and said, "If you are still here when we come back we will see about it." Then they went about their business. Toward evening that same farmer that saw me the day before came along and asked if I had lain "out in that storm last night?"

"I had to, because I could not walk," I said.

"Do you want to come with me?" I asked Father and He said I could go. I answered then, "I will." I hopped to the wagon and got on and he drove. After a long time we came to the house and they gave me some luncheon of corn bread and bacon which they had left from former meals, until she prepared supper. He brought me some turpentine for liniment, but Father said. "Don't use it. You will walk tomorrow."

I told them then that I could not use liniment because then they would think that it healed me. They looked at me suprised and did not say anything, but watched.

The next morning when I got up I walked and have walked ever since, though it pained me always till I reached the Hot Springs. In three weeks after I was taken to jail in Hot Springs the swelling was gone.

The first day I walked eighteen miles and waded the Illinois river. Oh, that water was cold. On the other side I camped and made my first fire. The next day I came to a house and Father said "Go in here." They received me well and gave me to eat. Then the man said, "You are in bad shape. If you will, you can stay with us this winter." I said, "I wish I could, but I have to get to Hot Springs."

Then the woman spoke up, "With that foot? Never! You'll never get to Fort Smith, and if you do, it will be minus one foot!"

"But I will get to Hot Springs with both feet," I said.

"I don't believe it," she said. But she did not know as much as I did.

On I went, being in the flint district. In the evening I passed the last houses and came into a canyon. Then for fifteen miles there were no houses or anything. I slept in the canyon that night, and kept going. At last I came to a creek, and when I had crossed it I saw a couple of houses. Father said, "Go there," They were Indians and they gave me to eat. I camped a little farther along and kept on going. At last I came to the neighborhood of Fort Smith. I came to the bridge, never dreaming it was a toll bridge. When I reached a little house the man had just hung out a lantern. I said, "Good evening, sir." He said, "Good evening," and I walked on, and never thought farther, but when I was about the middle of the bridge it burst upon me that it was toll bridge.

So you see Father managed to get me over the bridge without money, for He put the pity in that man's heart. He let that poor unfortunate, barefooted and bareheaded, go over without price. When over the bridge I went first to the left, then to the right, then to the left again. I passed a few stores and saloons, when a fellow said, "Oh, John, look-a-here." But I was gone by that time. It seemed to me I was in a railroad yard. I followed it to the cotton compress, turned to the right, came again to the railroad. It was so dark I could hardly see the road. I came several times to woods, then clearings, then to woods. Then I wanted to sleep in those woods. I said, "It was warm here. I can't find any better place. I am tired and exhausted. But Father said, "You have to go and ask for shelter." Oh, but I begged Him not to make me go; to let me sleep where I was. But I had to go or disobey. I went on and came to the Little Rock road with telegraph poles. I turned to my right, and on the left was a place with such big fires I supposed it was a brick yard, and on I went. At last Father said, "That is the place."

I said right away, "They! They will not give me shelter! It is of no use to go in. Me? A ragged tramp, barefooted and bareheaded!"

"But I want you to go."

"Well, if you want me to go I will," and opened the gate and went up to the proch. I rang the bell. a middle-aged woman came to the door. She had a lamp in her hand. Looking at me she said, "What do you want?"

"Can I have shelter for the night?"

"We never give shelter to any one."

I said, "All right. Good night," and went away. Then I had to go back to the place where I wanted to lie down at first, a long five-mile walk in the cold. I fixed a bed by raking leaves together with my fingers in a wash. I made no fire, for it was too close to the city. After lying down it began to rain and I complained to Father. But He said, "It will soon stop." It did. I slept pretty well that night.

He took me through the woods the next morning and, when five miles north, I came to two houses. I met a man splitting wood and asked for food. He asked questions and I told him. Then he told his wife to give me to eat. Then to pass through the city was hard for me. But when I reached the south side there was an oak grove, and a tent there in which was a tinker. Father said, "Ask for a drink and rest here till I tell you to go." I rested an hour and a half and Father gave the word, and I went. After a while a man came along with a wagon and asked me to ride, and Father said, "Yes." Then I understood why I had to wait with the tinker. And we also met the chain gang working the Little Rock road, and you understand the rest, for the time had not yet come. We talked of many things, and he told me he was hauling hay to the bishop. And when we came to the road we stopped and I walked on. I had a second invitation to ride, and then just before dark I came to a place and Father said, "Ask for something to eat." I went and found the doors wide open and nobody there. But Father said, "Sit down and wait." After a while the people came home and I asked the lady for something to eat, and she asked me to sit down till she cooked the meal. And I stayed all night, and after breakfast I walked away.

I came near a house which stood beside the river, and the whole household was outdoors. And the man questioned me. I told him and he said, "That is a novelty in America." I crossed the bridge and met a man on horseback, who questioned me. I told him I was guided by the Father. And he said, "You are crazy," and laughed and rode away. On I went and slept on the side of a hill. Next morning again I went, and it began to rain slowly, but I kept going. Finally I came to a little place and in the store they questioned me. They wanted me to stay, but the time was up and I had to go in the rain. When five miles out Father told me to go to a house and get something to eat and they cooked especially for me. The house stood on the left hand of the road. Then again on I went in the rain. It rained steadily all day. As night approached He took me to a house to ask for shelter, but they refused. Then into another house, they did the same thing. I was wet, cold and weary. I tried to make a fire, but could not. On I walked in the darkness and rain, when I came to a house. Those windows were lit up. The light and warm looked so cheerful and inviting, and then I said to Father, "Will you let me ask for shelter here? I know they will receive me kindly." But He said, "No," and I could not disobey, and kept on walking, footsore, in the mud and sharp stones, and barefooted. At 11 at night I could no more — I was exhausted. I said to Father, "I can no more." Not finding a fit place to lie down, I wrapped the wet blanket about me and sat against an oak tree all night. Oh, but I was sight next morning. Like a leaf in the wind did I shiver and my teeth chattered, my feet ached and I was hungry. Father then said, "Go over to that house near and they will give you to eat." I ate the bacon, hot corn bread and coffee, but I still shivered and could not get warm. I stayed a while to dry myself and then went on in the rain. But Oh, my poor feet — they were so sore I could hardly walk! I complained so much and asked if I could not wrap old rags around my feet, and He told me, "In the next house I take you to, you ask for them and they will be given you." At last I came to the place and went in. I asked for food and a young girl about eighteen gave me to eat. And I asked for rags for my feet and she gave me a pair of stockings; and on I went, happy as a lark.

I passed what they call Dutch creek, near Danville, and there I had to climb a terrible mountain. When I reached the top I wanted to camp, but Father told me to keep on going, that he wanted me to go to a certain house and ask for shelter. My feet were sore, though I had the stockings, and how painful in the night on those stones and gravel! When I reached that house the man said, "Go to the next door; they will give you a bed for twenty-five cents. I have no room." So I went away. After a while I camped, built a fire, and hunted a stone for a pillow. The night went on. When I reached a farm house the next day the woman gave me lots of corn bread and bacon. She asked questions. I told her I healed the sick, but will do greater healing in time to come. She said she had been sick, and was yet. I told her she would get better. Her name was Mrs. Kirk. And I walked away. After I had passed the last house in the village and right foot hurt dreadfully, and had all day. I could hardly stand on it. So Father told me to stop and make a fire. The wind was bitter cold, but I had the forest to protect me. Toward evening the man that lived in the last house came along and asked me how I felt. I told him I was disabled. The foot was badly swollen. He asked when I had food. "That same morning," I told him. He answered, "I will go get you milk and corn bread," and when he returned, told me if it rained to come to his house. I thanked him for his kindness, and he added, "Come to breakfast tomorrow, for this is the last house for twelve miles."

The night passed all right, and Father healed my foot again. Though I suffered I could walk by morning, and accepted the invitation to breakfast. I thanked them for the food, and went on through terribly rough mountain roads. During my walk Father told me to stop at the third house and get something to eat. There I stayed two days and nights, and they wanted me to stay longer. But I had to go about Father's work. It was very cold, but on I went for days through woods and mountains, and camped again in the forest, near a house; but I could not enter. It began to rain at 11 o'clock and kept it up all night. But this time I had plenty of wood and a good fire. In the morning Father said, "Go to this house and they will give you to eat." But it kept on raining. Father said, "Go; it does not matter if it does rain," and He took me in the mountain where it poured down all day. I was walking up and down the mountains in rocks, thorns, mud — no trail, no road, a lonely country and night coming on. I stopped almost in despair. "I don't care if I do die, but — only you will have no one to do your work." And there I lay down in the water all night, in the forest of big pine trees, and so cold! When morning came at last I did not know if I had any feet or not. Oh! Then I cried, but I had to go. After the sun began to shine I crawled to a pine tree for support. With my hands I raised one foot. After awhile I raised the other foot. I dragged myself up and after awhile could walk. Again I went on in the direction He told me. By 1 o'clock in the afternoon I came to the very same place where I started from in the morning of the day before. I had rather have had a thrashing; but Father works his plans though you may not understand. They gave me again to eat and I went on.

I waded creeks and the waters were very high, but in the evening I came to a party of traders in camp. I asked to stay with them. They gave me breakfast next morning. I then went over the mountains for Hot Springs, crossing a big creek, and as I reached a house He told me to go and get food. And after that at night I came to a house and the man said his wife was sick and would not give me to eat, but to go on to the next house, which proved to be empty; so I camped. On I went and next day came to the big creek. Oh! was that water cold? I complained and said, "Will this never stop? I am now getting stiff as an old stage horse. You heal others but you don't heal me." The sun began to shine, but my knees were painful. As I began to get better, suddenly I came to the river that empties into the Washita, and the waters ran high. Then He took me over a trail just at the mount where it ran into the Washita. I rolled up my trousers as far as I could and in I went. The first thing I knew I dropped down and the water was in my mouth, and no bottom! Then I struck out to swim. I tried several times, but no bottom. Then after awhile I found it with my feet and walked out, wet, cold and shivering from head to foot. Then I remembered the matches were in my vest pocket, and they too were wet. Then I said to Father, "Surely I will freeze to death here tonight." And as I lamented I had reached the top of the bank. However, I commenced raking leaves together and hunting dry wood, and, to my great astonishment, the first match I struck I had fire; and nobody will ever know how happy I was! Then I gathered more wood, for the night was upon me, and those wet, sticky clothes! I got wood enough at last and began to dry my clothes upon me, which took nearly all night.

At daybreak I was up and had my blankets rolled ready to start, but Father said, "Wait." I stayed by the fire, for those things have always a reason. He had promised that I should be in Hot Springs that night, and it was yet twenty miles away. I was not able to walk it in a day. That was out of the question — but He held His promise. I was in Hot Springs that night — and I did heal. As I was debating, two farmers came along. Seeing me by the fire they came to warm. They asked me questions. I answered. One farmer said:

"You can follow the wagon and I will carry you over the creeks; they are swollen. Then you won't have to wade."

I thanked him for his kindness and tried very hard to follow his wagon, but could no more. He stopped, waited and proposed this:

"If you give me your blanket and strap I will carry you to Hot Springs and give you two meals."

I asked Father what to do. He said, "Yes, do it." I gave him my bed and he told me to get up on his wagon saying, "There is the grub box. I suppose you are hungry."

We reached the Springs at dark and I went to the postoffice for my mail, but it was closed, In the dark I went away from the main streets, down a broad one to the south and reached a corner where a creek runs south. On a road to the right, in the woods, suddenly I came upon a house with a bonfire, and the children dancing around the fire. But as soon as they saw me they ran yelling into the house. I stood still till the man and woman came out with a lamp. They asked me what I wanted and I told them I was looking for someone. They asked the name and I told them I could not remember. The women then told me I was lost; that there were people living up the canyon. I turned and went back, much disconcerted, because I could not understand what Father was doing with me. But He said I would heal, and I believe. I must wait His time and I knew He would straighten things out. When I go and He said, "Straight up the canyon," and I had to climb that mountain in the night; and, at the top, I was to stop. Oh! was it cold? No fire! No blanket even! And the wind was blowing bitter cold. I begged and prayed to be taken to some warmer place, and I complained:

"Father, you can if you will, though I can't see."

At last He permitted me to get up and directed me in the dark to a gully in which were leaves, and in those I slept and felt better. Daylight came and with it the sunshine that warmed me up. I combed my hair and was mending my clothes with white twine string, when suddenly a young man came upon me, and I had not noticed his approach.

"Have you slept here?"

"Yes," I said.

"I don't want to hurt you, but have you had anything to eat?"

"No."

"Well, I will send you something."

After a while a boy brought me hot biscuit and bacon and coffee — and if that didn't taste good! Think of that poor, cold stomach! In a few minutes he came back with a pair of overalls and shoes, saying:

"If you go into the city this way you will be arrested. It is too bad the shoes are too small."

I thanked him, but went to the city and to the postoffice and got some paper and letters.

I was discouraged, and Father said, "Go out of the city." And I was very glad to go.

I went back to the main street greatly troubled. I was attending to my own business, neither was I lounging, when suddenly I felt a hand on my shoulder. Turning, there stood a colored policeman.

"Where are your shoes."

"My feet are so swollen I can't wear any."

"Where is your hat?"

"I don't wear any."

"Then," said the police, "Come along." As we walked, a white policeman came up, and between the two I walked the streets to the station, followed by hundreds of people. When there I was searched, and they knew my name, from the mail. They asked questions and I told them. For that they put me in the calaboose. And that was the first time I ever saw that sight. Presently the constable came and said to come with him to a better place. And that better place was the county jail. On reaching there they made me wait till the sheriff arrived, and then they questioned me again, and I told them I was guided by the Father.

"Can we not see that Father?" said the sheriff.

"You may see Him before you know it," I answered. Whereupon he used an expression which no man should use to another. Then the spirit came upon me and I gave him such a look that he did not want another. Turning to his deputy he said:

"Take him to the cage. He is as crazy as a bed bug." So into the cage I went.

The prisoners all eyed me, the news having traveled ahead of me that I was crazy. After being in the cage a while I went over to a corner and began washing out some handkerchiefs, when what is known as the "Kangaroo Court" went into session, as it does immediately on the arrival of a new prisoner. The sheriff of this strange court came over to where I was and said,

"They want you over here in the court."

His name was Will Singleton. The judge was Eugene Donahue. All the rest of the prisoners were at the mock trial. Outside the cage was a railroad engineer, he having been arrested upon a devilish charge and robbed. Then they say, "He has to have lawyers to get him out!"

Well, there was the court in session, but I would not go. They sent their sheriff a second time, but I just smiled at him and kept on washing. Then the judge gave a decision:

"That fellow has just got to come up. If he don't we will knock sense into him!" And he ordered a poor little colored boy, eleven years old, thus:

"You go tell that crazy fellow to come up here, and if you don't go you will get a licking." So that poor little boy came over to me crying pitifully and sobbed out:

"They want you up there." I looked at the little unfortunate and said, "I will go." I took his hand and he led me over to their meeting. They told me to sit down, and I accepted the chair offered. Then the judge said:

"You are charged with jail breaking — or breaking into jail — and are fined one dollar and a half." I told the judge I had no money.

"You have a watch," said the judge. I asked Father what I should do. He said not to give it to them. So I told them they could not have my watch.

"This court decides you are to have one hundred and fifty lashes with a rubber hose six feet long and an inch and a quarter in diameter. Now are you willing to give up that watch?"

"No," I answered.

The judge then delegated six men to take hold of me and Dee, a fourteen-year-old boy, to lash me. So they all took hold of me. The lashing had stared, when suddenlty the spirit came over me. With one powerful jerk I was free. They all had disappeared, and when I looked around all had fled to their cells but one, who was sitting and had not said a word; and I went back to my washing. Then they all came out again and court was called and convened again. When in session I was called up and went. Charley Williams — for he was a good man — stepped forward and said:

"I will pay this man's fine." I asked Father and He said, "No." So

I told the court:

"I can't see why this man should pay my fine. You have asked for my watch and you can not have it." Then there was a dead silence. No one spoke. You could have heard a pin drop.

Suddenly I was seized and laid on the table, and Singleton, a tall, raw-boned colored fellow, six feet high, angry because I broke away from them the first attempt, was beating me and, he being mad, it is needless to say the lashes came down with all his might. Williams, who was holding me and counting, said:

"Stop, that is enough!" when the hose struck me the fiftieth time.

I rose, sat down in the chair and wept bitterly. It seemed I was, indeed, forsaken now.

In time the eyes dried, and when I looked up the prisoners were all quietly watching me. Singleton broke the silence first, saying. "The officials are crazier than that man."

After I had been there three weeks the sheriff came up and, standing by the door, said:

"Have you any more sense than when you came in?"

"No more, no less," was out of my mouth before I knew it. But Father had always told me, "You will get out of jail when My time comes, not theirs. I will prepare things for you."

After that Father told me I could eat no meat, only vegetables and bread. So I told the man that brought in the meals, and he told me I would have to speak to the deputy sheriff. So I did. He asked the reason why, and I told. I was then healing among the prisoners, and he said. "All right." And this deputy sheriff was always good to me. After that it was always vegetables, bread and coffee.

One Sunday morning the Salvation Army people came up preaching and praying, and a Mrs. Washington said that in this glorious age, in this land of the free, no one was put in prison for his religious faith. She came only a few times and, like the rest of the prisoners, I was standing barefooted on the iron floor. But they asked no questions.

Some one came every Sunday. On a certain Sunday a young man came, and we talked, and I finally said:

"Why am I here? Because of my faith!"

"Why don't you get a lawyer to get you out?"

"I came in without a lawyer and I am going to get out without a lawyer!"

So the time passed. I was healing and everybody knew of it. Still the time passed, and I was kept in jail. But I knew when Father was ready He would get me out, for one night I had a dream. I thought I was out of jail in what looked like a modern house, a large house, and a bird came in by the window. It went in a second room and flew into a third; turned and came back and went out of the window which it had entered. When in the last room, or rather the first, where it came in, all cried out, "Catch it!" but it was out of the window before they could — the bird was gone.

In the morning I remembered my dream and understood. The Invincible, Invisible Hand had set to work to remove whatever was in my path.

Weeks after, some of the trusties got drunk and were put in the cage, and the deputy sherrif asked me if I wanted to work. Father said I could so I said, "Yes."

He opened the cage and out I came! Father said, "You work with all your might all your strength and all your power." And so I did. And for this the clerk of the jail called me "Cyclone" I was always quick, prompt, never behind time. I sawed and split wood, cleaned house, also the court house; also swept out the court house when court was in session. I washed dishes, and did anything and everything that could be done.

One day the deputy sheriff's wife asked me if they could hire me to work, I seemed to like it. I told her there wasn't money enough in all this world to hire me. But had I been a diplomat that was my second chance to escape, you see. But the time had not yet come, nor was I to get out by diplomacy.

One day I was sent for beer. I went and got them their beer and I met a colored woman that visited prisoners. She knew the manner and the reason I was put in jail and kept there. She said:

"Are you in jail yet?"

"Yes," I said, "but when Father's time comes I will get out. I don't know when."

I repeated this conversation on my return, to the deputy sheriff's wife. She told her husband and he, in turn, went to the sheriff and said:

"He's all right now. He has been detained long enough." So the sheriff called me to him and said:

"How would you like it if I would set you up in business?"

"I had a business once, but I had to give all away to do my Father's work."

"What is that work?" asked he.

"I know what it was last year, but I can not tell you what it will be this year;" and that settled that.

So there was my third chance to get out. I knew well the reason he did not give me my liberty. He was afraid. He was influenced by those lawyers who advised. "Hold on to that fellow."

So I kept on working with all my might, and on the last Sunday a lawyer was talking to the deputy sheriff's wife and I was cleaning the last windows. The lawyer said, "That fellow is just crazy to work! Just let him work."

The conversation was in a low tone of voice, but whatever I have to hear I will hear. And I heard it as plainly as if he had told it in my ear.

The next evening Father said. "Go!" and I did go, and am going yet.

The first night I slept on the other side of the mountains, north of Hot Springs. In the morning Father took me to the house of colored people, and they gave me to eat.

On I went, to the electric cars, into the mountains. And in the afternoon I passed through that little town beyond the mountains, and the first thing I knew I was at the same place I was at in the early morning. Then I began to worry and complain, though I knew they could not catch me. But I worried. On I went over the same ground only a little further west.

The next day I spent in the mountains, and the next, and Father said, "Now you have to walk, I will give you the strength." I kept on going till about half-past seven, and it was dark. I got on the road but did not notice till it stopped. I asked Father if I should go back and He said, "No, straight ahead." I came to a fence, and over I went straight on till I came to a road, and I asked, "Which way?" "To the left," He told me. That was southwest, toward Bluffton. I walked a while longer, then He said I could lie down, and took me a few hundred yards from the road to fallen trees.

And the next morning I got breakfast in a house where I had eaten before I went to Hot Springs. It was a blacksmith shop, and when I left, instead of following the road to Bluffton, I took to the left and into the mountains. For two days in those mountains I saw nothing but big trees, and walked from daylight till dark.

The third day I was on the Waldron & Hot Springs road, and Father took me into a house, and they gave me to eat.

I went on again toward Hot Springs, retracing my steps into the mountains. The next day I came to the same house by noon, and they again gave me to eat. Then to the north, on a road to the left into the mountains till dark. The following day I found the same road I had passed before, and had to go back on that to reach Waldron. Passed there in the night; on to Huntington and to the Indian Territory. I walked every day from thirty-five to forty-five miles until I reached the Territory.

After I had passed Huntington and was coming through the

mountains, I reached a place early in the afternoon. I was very, very hungry. Father said, "Go in here and ask." I went. The household were all out on the porch. The man was reading the Bible. I asked for something to eat. Looking up from the Bible, he said:

"Do you fellows think I am going to feed you?"

So I thanked him and went on, saying, "Father, you heard what that man said!" "Yes," He said, "but He is one of the mouth worshippers only. He never has fulfilled his prayers; but I wanted you to see how he is going to do with you. And now you are going to a house a little further on, and they do not pray, but they will give you to eat." When I came to the house He took me in and I asked, and they gave me. And they were old people at that.

Through the Territory I went, right and left, back and forward, up and down, everywhere, when one day He took me to a section house on the Missouri Pacific. It was at Folsom. The house is east of there. The people were very kind and good to me, and in the evening we were talking of spiritual things. And I said, "Did not Jesus say if we have faith only as large as a grain of mustard seed we can move mountains?"

One of the men said, "But that man is not living."

"Yes, he is living," I said, "and he is right before you. And some day, when Father gets ready, I will move mountains."

Afterwards I went on, and oh! for day I had a hard time! One night I was near to desperation, and I lay under a bush and cried like a child. I said, "Father, the world is too heavy for me. Oh! why did you not take somebody else to do the work?" and went to sleep. In the morning I felt stronger than ever, and went on and kept on.

On day I came to a section house on the railroad I was following. It was on a Sunday afternoon. I asked the woman for something to eat. She answered, "Yes, but go out and split wood."

"All right, madam. Where is the ax?"

I had eaten no food for twenty-four hours, so I kept splitting wood. She sent the lunch out to me and I ate it on the woodpile. Then began to split wood again. The man came out and said, "That's enough." I took the ax to where I got it. When leaving, I told them there are many sick around here, but if you have faith you will get well, and as I walked away the man said:

"You have a hard way to serve the Lord."

That was a hard road I had through Texas. One morning Father took me to a farmer and I asked for food. He replied:

"We have nothing to eat in this part of the country."

"You will have less before long," which answer angered him and he said:

"No back talk."

I crossed Red River and asked a section boss for a drink, and he refused me water to drink, even, and I was so thirsty in the heat.

When I came to Paris I was walking through in a hurry, and along the road there stood three so-called ladies, and one said to the other two, pointing toward me:

"What do you call that thing?"

I heard it at that distance, and, no need to say, for a moment I was wild. But I had to keep still. Father said, "Keep still; you will have your say some day, and there will be no back talk then. But you must bear the burden first." So on I went through Paris, and took the first cross road to the right towards Fort Worth. I believe it is the Texas Pacific. When I came to the 110th telegraph pole, Father said, "Go over to that house and they will give you to eat." For thirty-six hours I had not tasted food. He also said, "There are two in the house sick, but they will be well if they have faith." So I went and asked for food. The lady of the house gave it to me, and I told her what Father said. She was surprised. And when I had finished eating, her husband came and began to curse and damn, and said if he ever found me in that house again he would have me put me in jail. Father said, "Keep still. Don't answer. Don't speak." I had walked from the start of his talk, and shrunk from the abuse, and, when away alone, I cried and said, "Father, I am not to beg any more?"

I kept on walking in awful hunger, oh! What hunger! Toward a certain evening there was a storm in all four quarters, the wind blowing, and it began to rain. I prayed to Father to stop the storm. "I am so hungry now. How cold will I be all this night!" And the rain stopped. But it rained all around me at a radius of half a mile. I was lying in a corn field and Father said, "Go over to that house and ask for something to eat;" for I had been three days without anything.

When I reached the house, first came the dogs at me, and they did not call them back. They all came out from dinner and were sitting on the proch. One said scornfully:

"Did the dogs bite you?"

"Yes," I said, "they would if they only could," and I asked the man for something to eat.

"We are such a hungry set here that we eat everything up," at which they all began to hoot and laugh, and they shouted as far as I could hear. Oh! I could not describe to you my feelings! I told Father, "You have a lot of bad stewards. You have given full and plenty for all your children, but they can not get it. Some let it rot sooner than give a little to a poor and unfortunate. Instead of lifting him up they crush him."

On to Fort Worth, on the Texas Pacific to the freight yards. It was very dark and Father told me to lie down, because I was so ragged I would have been arrested in the day time. I often begged, "Let me work just long enough to earn clothes. I will then go again." But always came the same answer:

"Follow me. When I want you to have clothes you will have clothes. When I want you to have shoes you will have them. When I want you to have food you will have it. Follow me."

At 11 at night He woke me up, I had slept so long at the old round house; and on I went, nor did I meet a living soul. Then I reached the freight yard; to the right over the bridge, then south to another bridge. Father said, "Go down there; that is your road." It was very dark. I could not see the bottom, but down I went. I found two roads, and He told me the left. I found I was on the Texas Pacific. A few miles further I reached a clump of trees and Father said, "Lie down and rest." I had a sleep, though it rained. On I went the next day. Oh! What rain! I seemed wet to the bone. On through Weatherford. Slept in a ditch of water that night. Out of doors every night. No clothes, no food, no bed. It was just horrible, terrible! But I had to go. There was no going back, because then I could neither live nor die. My bridges were burned behind me. And I tell you I am going to do this work, and it will be done right.

Next day over the Canadian river, into a mountain, over a canyon spanned by an iron bridge. Then on to a high plateau. After many miles' walk there is a little town, and at one house Father said, "Go, and ask for food." There were little girls and a deaf young man. I asked for something to eat. The little girls encouraged the dog to go after me, and that was the first time a dog had touched me. Many dogs had tried to bite me, but every one, after he tried, seemed ashamed of himself. But that one tore my clothes. I went back to their house to get something to sew it up. I had neither thread nor needle. I asked for them and she handed me them with such contempt!

I thanked her and went my way. I went under a bush to sew up my clothes, and complained. I said to Father, "There has not been a dog for all this time that could touch a thread on my body. But this dog could not tear my overalls if you did not want him to. But I suppose you thought I was not ragged enough."

Came to Cisco. Left there at sunrise. Passed Albany in the dead of night, then on to Throckmorton. I had gone about half a mile and was so tired Father said, "Lie down. You will heal in this place."

Next morning He told me to stay there. "Somebody who is sick will come along and ask questions. Tell them you heal." I said, "If you make me stay today under this bush I will be in jail tonight."

"Yes," He told me.

At 11 o'clock a man came to me. He was sick and asked questions. I told him, but he did not believe. He went away and at about 5 the sheriff, with several men, came along. At first they thought I was crazy, but soon found out I was not. And that sheriff and judge were good men. They gave me to eat. I slept in jail. Gave me breakfast and let me go my way.

A man called me back and asked me if I would heal him. I sat down on a store stoop and held his hands about twenty minutes, and during that period the stoop was full of people, and they were laughing and giggling. I stopped and asked how he felt, and he said, "Better." I turned to the crowd. I could hardly keep back the tears, and I said, "In three days you will have more faith than you have now," and I walked away and passed through Haskell, Anson, and here I threw away that shirt.

On to Abilene, Colorado and Van Horn. Went to a mountain. Passed a section house, and three miles from it I found a shirt. The day before I had found a spool of thread. So I mended it, and had one to wear. The following day I came to a section house. It was dark, and the section boss was an Irishman. I asked Him for something to eat and he said so cheerfully:

"Why did you not come sooner?"

"If I could have I would." Then he asked me to eat, and he asked questions. I told him, and he said:

"You know your business. I know mine. I never criticise any one. What they tell me I believe."

We talked happily, and that evening he gave me a pair of overalls. Then again I looked a little better.

A few days after that I said to Father, "That coat looks shabby enough, but I suppose you will get me a coat some time. He said. "Yes."

So I threw away the old one and passed through El Paso, then to Strauss on the Southern Pacific.

A Mexican gave me three days' rest. His sister was sick in El Paso. On again to Aden, and another three days' rest.

On again to Deming, Benson, Tucson, Maricopa, Gila Bend, Yuma, Mammoth Tank. I healed among the Mexicans and there was one section boss who ordered me away.

I passed Indio, Colton; and here a young man gave me a coat. At Puente del Molino I started to heal ranchers. Also at Old Mission,

Lordsburg, Azusa, San Gabriel, Payona. Stayed one night in Los Angeles. Back to San Gabriel. And when two months and three days were passed I had to go onward.

On Thanksgiving night I walked down to Pomona and Colton. When a few miles outside the latter I passed a fellow. I felt tired. My feet were blistered terribly. So I took a rest. After a while he came along and passed the time of day, talked and asked questions, and I answered. When I started he followed, saying he too was going that way. And then he said he was deaf. I healed him of his deafness and fed him as long as he was with me. Before we reached San Diego I gave him six dollars to help him till he should get work.

When walking one day, as the magnitude of the work necessary to be done was being unfolded to me gradually, I said to Father:

"I have not will power enough for such a terrible work such as you tell me I must do." And he said:

"No, not now, but you will have pretty soon."

So when we reached San Diego the boat was gone, and it was very late, and I said, "Let us go to a restaurant." They were Denver people, but they had no rooms, so took us to the Forrester House. We had a room with two beds, and I paid the bills. I asked Father what I should do with the money I then had — put it under the mattress or leave it in my pocket. Father told me to leave it in my pocket. I obeyed and fell into a deep sleep. In the morning twelve dollars were gone, but the man stayed right there. I left and he wanted to shake hands. But I went north of San Diego and spent Sunday and Monday, returning in time to take Tuesday's boat for San Francisco.

At 11 I left there and took the road to San Jose, then to Niles and Tracy. And during all this continental tramp I had no blanket. I asked Father if I could not buy a blanket and some cotton cloth to make a little tent. He said I could, and I passed on to Lathrop, north of Merced, and met another man. I had made the tent and it was finished. I had bought a hatchet and Father said:

"You travel with that fellow. He is all right." But I did not know in which way.

I had also bought fifty pounds of flour. The next day camped about five miles south of Merced at an abandoned ranch. There were here two young fellows going to the mountains prospecting. In the evening we were sitting in the little tent, for it was raining, and we had a small fire at the opening. They went off to the barn to sleep and I was left in the tent with my fellow. I had healed him of fever, too. I said to Father:

"Shall I take off my clothes and make pillow with them?"

"Yes," he said. So I took them off and rolled them up and lay down. After a while the fire got low, so I got up to get some wood that was lying at my feet to fix the fire. While I was fixing the fire he shot out of the tent just like a mad man. I wondered what was the matter with him. Had he gone crazy? But I kept on fixing the fire till Father thought he was far enough. Then He let me know I was robbed of everything. I started after him, but it was dark and I could not see. Then I went back and hunted around. He had been in such a hurry that he left his own clothes, and I used them; but I would rather have had mine. I saw he had put the hatchet on his side of the bed. I knew he was armed with a six-shooter. With the two, he had prepared for fight to the finish. But Father knew his heart, and that was the reason I had to undress and make a convenient pillow of the clothes; and He gave him the chance to rob me without violence. Because Father also knew that I was not afraid either of him or the hatchet; and he would have had to do something to rob me by force. But, well, he had my all and I said to Father: "You gave me that little money and you took it away again. You have perfect right. But you starve me — the one who does your will and your work the best I know how. Then you feed the robbers. I understand. You want to give temptation again and try me again by hunger, cold and carrying this awful burden, heavy enough for a mule. Now I am made a beast of burden."

I was carrying fifty pounds of flour, a tent, tent pole and pins, blanket, hatchet, frying pan, a coat and water pail.

I found my clothes the next day, but later on gave them to a poor man, keeping the coat for use later. My bill of fare was, day after day, flour and water as long as it lasted. I had salt, but soon that was gone and I had no way to buy more. Father said I could not beg. I could not disobey and yield to temptation, for then I would not have been true to the will of the Father. So I had to make every sacrifice, and kept going day after day with that burden, that heavy weight. In rain and shine I had to go and overcome all things. Such trails and preparations bring results, and they came fast.

One night, after terrible suffering, I sat down on a railroad tie, as I had often, and cried. It was only two months before that I had said, "Father, I have not will power enough to do the terrible work you have planned." But now I said: "I have will power enough to spare!"

Of course these two men who have robbed me are not the only robbers there are on this earth. The whole of society, the way it is organized, is nothing but robbery, legalized by man-made laws, hence lawful robbery; and the schemers take advantage and always rob the honest and faithful. Have they not, through those legalized robberies, torn up families, made tramps, paupers and prostitutes? Who are responsible for such a state of affairs? Who made the laws and then betrayed the trust which the nation gave; turned and robbed the masses for the benefit of the few?

On I went on that terrible walk, for the sake of humanity. I stood firm against all temptation of all the devils, in spirit as well as in the flesh. Today the saints and devils are all living. The saints generally are trampled into the dust because, through honesty, they are unsuccessful in business as well as in governmental affairs.

At last the flour gave out, but Father provided. A man came and bought the coat for two dollars, and I went to a farmer and bought wheat for twenty-five cents, and some salt. With the boiled wheat I walked over the Alpines, to Moraine and six miles east of Barstow I pitched the tent and stopped for two weeks.

Father said I would heal and I did a little, but for lack of faith I could not heal more. They could not believe that a tramp could heal. In two weeks I went on my journey. The wheat was gone and I bought flour and bacon.

When east of Fenner I met a freight train wrecked. The night was upon me and I camped beside the wreck. There were many men working. I asked the section boss for some water and he told me to help myself. I left all my things in the tent and went a few hundred yards for water. When I came back the pocket knife was gone, stolen by someone who worked on that wreck. It had been given to me. But I had to keep still, as usual, saying nothing.

After I had walked about a mile the spirit came over me and I promised Father that I would never rest as long as there was a thief, liar or hyprocrite on the face of the earth. I said, "Just as sure as I can smash his tent pole, in Father's time will I crush the serpent which has his coils around the world, and which nothing can break but the Creator himself!"

Sure enough, the pole split lengthwise from end to end, in two, and I wired it up at one end and tied it with a shoe string at the other.

Two days after, I was making bread in the frying pan, and as I turned over the dough the handle broke off and down went the dough into the sand. You see everything was going to smash, and now I must be like a chicken and eat sand all the time. That afternoon I passed The Needles. I camped along the railroad, in a draw. The day following, walked on. On the bridge the wind nearly blew me off. Got a little water. Went on a little way, cooked flour and water, and kept on my lone journey.

I walked late at night, and the left foot gave out. It was so swollen next day I could not walk. When about four miles from Franconia, the day after, the track walker passed and we talked. He said, "It is hard luck to be without water." No one passed the next day. The third day the track walker passed again, and asked, in astonishment, "Have you had no food or water since Sunday?"

"No, sir."

"Well, I will go and see the section boss and ask what he can do about you."

In about an hour the hand car came along and they gave me water. I cooked the paste again and was two days near the section house, and was all right. The reason of that was Father wanted to try the faith of the section boss and see if he would help a poor and unfortunate, lying beside the road. Had he not come the third day I would have lain there five days without water or food, and then Father would have healed the foot and given me strength to walk away.

I had often such experiences, though I have not mentioned them all, and the people passed by except two — like the Pharisee and the Levite.

I passed through Kingman and there brought five cents' worth of crackers and five cents' worth of cheese, and that was the last of the money.

At Hackberry I had to stay for days. I had enough water for one day after arriving; then went the other three without food or water. When I left I could hardly walk. But when the pack was on my back the strength came. Father showed me a house and told me to go in and ask for food. I did, and the woman told me to split wood first. I did it gladly, and the food tasted so good!

On the journey I passed Peach Springs, Ash Fork, Williams and Flagstaff in the night, going up toward the Grand Canyon. I camped near Flagstaff, the next day went up the road to get over the mountain. At a farm Father told me to go in and ask for something to eat. The lady very kindly gave it to me, and asked questions. Among many other things I told her, "The day is near when all the faithful will live together," and she answered:

"Oh! I read those things, but I don't believe them any more."

"The day comes, and you will see!" I just said to her, thanking her for her kindness.

As I journeyed the road was terrible. Snow and slush ankle-deep. Every now and then waded creeks full of ice and snow. Late one afternoon came to the foot of the mountain where there were great houses and barns, and Father said:

"Go ask for shelter."

I met the man at the door and asked simply for shelter, but he refused. Then he asked where I was going.

"Up toward the Grand Canyon."

"Well, why didn't you go down around the mountain?"

"If Father wanted me to have gone around the mountain I would have gone, but He wanted me to go over the mountain, and I am going over the mountain."

"I would not go over that mountain for fifty dollars," said the man.

"I am going for less," and I started off, bidding him good-night. After I had gone a short distance he called me back, saying kindly, "You can stay here."

I laid my burden down. He invited me in and made a good fire. I dried my feet, for I had walked all afternoon ankle-deep though snow and slush. My old shoes were so worn that my toes were sticking out, and I had so socks. He began to question me as to what I was doing in that forest at that time of year, and I told him I was doing spiritual work. He gave a hearty laugh and said:

"Excuse me, old man, for laughing at you, but there is no one living down in this forest, and you will die of hunger."

"There must be somebody living there, otherwise I would not have to go. As for dying, I will not, for the Father has prepared a way. No doubt I will have to suffer, but that is all. I have to go."

He gave me supper and breakfast and the lady next morning gave me a big lunch. I went up and up the snow-capped mountain. On the summit the snow covered the bushes, and every step I fell to my knees. Every time I drew out my feet the shoes were filled with snow and ice. The wind blew a gale, and in a few hours my feet were so cold they had no feeling. When I laid my hands on them there was no sensation, but on I went.

After a while I saw smoke, and had to reach the shanty. When I got there I asked leave to warm myself. In two hours the feet were warm again. Out into and through the snow again, and after a while I came to another cabin.

A man there was digging a ditch through the snow to save his lot from getting under water as it did when the snows melted rapidly. But it was turning cold very fast and began snowing. When I reached him I asked for shelter. He told me to go in and warm, and presently came himself and asked questions. I explained my mission and, like the others, he said warningly:

"There is nobody living in this forest, and you will starve to death."

"There must be some one; otherwise I would not have to go. I will suffer, of course, but I will not die."

Then he asked about provisions, saying:

"I have only a little, as this is not my winter home. I simply came up this morning to look after the ditches. I brought enough for myself only."

I told him not to be troubled about food; for I go without for days, but Father sustains me and it does not matter.

"Well, if you do not eat, neither will I. If you can fast and often for so long, I can for once. We will eat what I have for our breakfast together."

We lay down to sleep. Oh! Did it blow and snow all night?

He went home the next day in the snow storm and our roads went part way together. But the trail was terrible for me, for Father took my strength away. I could not follow, but when ahead he would wait for me, for he would not leave me behind in that awful snow storm. Presently he said:

"Take off that burden, that pack on your back, and I will carry it for you, so you can follow." But Father took more strength away still, and I could do not better than before. When we reached the forks of the road he waited and said:

"This is my way, to the southeast. You had better come home with me, for on the road you propose to go there is one ranch only five miles from here, with no one there probably, and nothing again for twenty-five miles."

I thanked him for his help, but had to go my own road. When I reached the ranch there was a sheep herder and he invited me to stay. And I did.

Then to the north, to Smoky Station. Turned west to a sheep camp. Father said:

"Ask for work as a sheep herder." I did.

"Have you ever herded sheep before?"

"No, sir, but others do, and I can, if you give me the chance," was my reply.

"I need a man in a couple of weeks, but not now. You can stay around camp till I go to town and we will see when I get back."

So he went off and returned in a week or so, and then said:

"You do not know how to herd sheep and I've no time to teach you. So I have no need of you."

But I made good use of those ten days in various ways. I got on to the inside of the sheep herding business.

Under the guidance of the Father I went north and met two other sheep herders, and they said I would starve to death if I went that way. But I gave the usual answer, that I would not die, that Father would keep me one way or another. When He wants me to go He has a way prepared.

I went on and came to another sheep camp, and again asked for work. The owner, however, did not speak encouragingly.

"I have," he said, "such a small herd I could not give you much wages."

"It does no matter. Money is no object to me."

Then he explained that he had also offered it for sale and was waiting an answer, but said I could stay there meantime. In due season they were turned over into a large herd; but he told me to stay for shearing and work around camp, for they had corrals to build and needed rails; that one herder might leave and I could take his place. So I cooked, made bread, split wood, split rails and did whatever was to be done. He had a letter to bring the herd to Flagstaff, to be sheared there, and to turn the herd over to another party. We went and delivered the sheep. They were sheared and dipped. The 1st of May the herder left and they asked me to herd the sheep till they could get a herder. The 8th of May, at night, they relieved me. So I was in and about the sheep camps from April 1 to the date given.

Then began again the continental walk, through Winslow and Gallup; also the miles northeast of Fort Wingate, in the Navajo reservation. Five days with Chief Ho-ka-ni-ridge, and from there came back to the Atlantic & Pacific railroad, and through the hot sands and sun I came, in due season, to Las Lunas, New Mexico, in July, 1895.

FRANCIS SCHLATTER.

No relief from the oppressive strain of this mournful account was vouchsafed by the writer; we are permitted no breathing spell, such as a division into chapters would have granted. Yet loyalty to the trust forbids any changes in the manner of its arrangement.

The magnitude and mystery of this agony, the monotony of the recital of suffering, are more difficult of interpretation as his record abruptly closes than in this beginning. His halting manner of writing, the day when he sat at the desk a while, then getting up saying, "Not today," proved that the memory of the horrible ordeal was at times insufferable. Other days a page would be accomplished. Once he grasped his head with both hands fairly moaning as he exclaimed, "God! was I cold? Was I not?" After this reminiscence of his walk through the slushy ice of the Arizona mountains, from day to day the postponement was steady until such time as he rallied strength to record it for the public to read. The frequent suggestion that he should elaborate and explain it, as he did in conversation, was dismissed by:

"That is enough. That will show them. I walked for the world," adding, with a look of infinite pity and tenderness: "But have they done their best always? No! How have you felt when robbed? There would have been no necessity for me to go, to walk, had they lived good lives. I had to suffer to for humanity. If they don't recognize it, I am indifferent. They can accept it or reject it; I don't care. Father doesn't ask others to fast, to walk, to suffer. My walk was the fire I went through for the world. I was preparing."

The five months barefooted on the iron floors of the Arkansas jail, the sands of Texas, the death-dealing cold of the Arizona mountains are trifles compared with his endurance of the vast stretches on the Mojave desert, where many have perished. He entirely ignored the physical features of that region, features which the few surviving travelers have described. A man who was lost on this desert says: "I existed for three weeks without eating. The pink-throated lizards, the river without water, the dry sand that gave nutrition to naught save the cacti, were my world. When asked how I lived I replied, 'In despair.'" And the celebrated tribute to the Colorado desert by Madge Morris may define ever more clearly the unendurable trip made by the Healer, with only wheat and water, meanwhile carrying that burden:

"Thou brown, bare breasted, voiceless mystery,
Hot Sphinx of Nature, cactus-crowned!
What hast thou done?
Unclothed and mute as when the groans of chaos turned
Thy naked, burning bosom to the sun.
The mountain silences have speech, the rivers sing —
Thou answerest never unto anything.

Thy sharp mescal shoots up a giant stalk,
Its century of yearning to the sun-burnt skies,
And drips rare honey from the lips
Of yellow, waxen flowers, and dies!
Some lengthwise, sun-dried shapes of feet and hands,
And thirsty mouths pressed on the sweltering sands
Mark, here and there, a gruesome, graveless spot.
Where some one drank they scorching hotness and is not.
God must have made thee in His anger — and forget!"

But the Healer followed, as he heard the command, no matter how much agony obedience involved. And he believes still more misery, pain and oppression will be necessary to bring men, to force men, to think themselves out of present conditions. When the commands were more than he could endure he sat upon a railroad tie and wept; the vision of Jesus carrying the Cross being the frequent and only support and encouragement he needed, and "Father would then give me the strength to endure to the end," were his words.

Every day in January he narrated in detail this superhuman exploit, made doubly interesting by the relating, also, of all that the Father said to him. It was somewhat startling one day to hear the following reminiscence:

"'Father, shall I ever marry?'

"'Yes,' He told me, 'but you can not choose your bride.'"

Any ordinary mind could grasp the mighty meaning in a flash, and I replied instantly:

"Humanity is your bride, but you did not choose her."

"Father says you are right," was the laconic response.

From that hour all thought of sects, cults, schisms or churches passed away, and the greatest humanitarian on the planet abode there. But every expression of sympathy, or rebellion at the idea of his unceasing sorrow was quietly corrected by these words:

"It all has an object. The Kingdom is near. It will be a spiritual congregation of souls, highly developed through the unfoldment of many rebirths. None can enter the Kingdom who has had less than ten good lives. The chosen ones are the highest, purest, best."

If the reader deems unnecessary the strong language use during the retirement on the ranch when giving an analysis of the economic and political conditions, he may find it fully justified by reading John, 5:29 or 8:44, and many other of Jesus' sayings too numerous for reference in this volume.

CHAPTER II.

THE FAST IN ALBUQUERQUE.

The excitement and the candid interest now prevailing in Denver over the appearance here of a man claiming to be Christ is, in a thousand ways, a fact of the widest significance to all capable of viewing its bearings without prejudice.

It is one of those facts that greatly illustrate the social conditions of a period, and vividly illuminate the yearnings of the impulses of the human heart. It is a fact which equally rebukes the self-complacency of institutional religion and the entrenched bigotry of science.

But this, of course, is all perceptible only to the broad view, and the broad view is not possible to the narrow mind. The ignorant will marvel, the shallow will quibble and fleer, and only the wise will take the facts of the case into their souls and reflect on their wide and pathetic significance — for there is a sublime and dramatic pathos in this Denver event, as in all scenes that reveal the yearnings of the human heart in their primary and guileless simplicity; such a sublime and dramatic pathos as is revealed to tender souls in the brief but luminous words, "Jesus wept."

From two thousand to five thousand people a day, of all creeds, all colors, and all social conditions, crowd to see this simple, devoted man who, by abandoning himself utterly to the uses of the Holy Spirit, has gained an amazing power to heal ailing flesh — to give sight to the blind, hearing to the deaf, speech to the dumb, suppleness to the palsied. They do not come because they believe he is Christ — not that exactly, in any case perhaps, and not that at all in most cases, certainly — but because the memory of Christ has left a basis for rational faith in such works. The modesty of his ways, the guileless earnestness, the utter selfsurrender to the Holy Spirit, inspire a prompt respect, a profound interest and a compassionating affection. It is impossible for any but a mind imbittered by bigotry or debased by licentiousness to question the purity and unselfishness of his spirit. To question his mental condition is quite another thing. But it is important to emphasize that, barring the claim that he is Christ reincarnated, his presence makes upon me, and I think upon all, the impression of an extremely simple but perfectly sane mind. As, however, his case is worthy of the most careful scientific observation, I should state that he has another form of what, rigidly regarded, appears to be illusion, in our present knowledge of the psycho-mental functions — he continually uses the expression, in describing the schooling he had gone through for this ministry of healing, "I had to" do this and "I had to" do that. Judicious inquiry, however, develops that this "had to" is not exactly a command from objective "voices," such as directed Joan of Arc, but simply a subjective impression of the Will of the Holy Spirit. This, of course, will be readily recognized as only a slightly exaggerated impression of a religious phase common to all who attempt to surrender the personal will, in any earnest measure, to the guidance of the Holy Spirit, as distinguished from those who try to govern their conduct by reason or principle solely.

While the cures effected by this interesting being are innumerable, unquestionable and, in many cases, surprising it would be an outrage upon truth and upon the man's simple and modest claims, to say that there is anything miraculous about them. Not all cases treated are cured or even appreciably alleviated, and none are cured instantly, though many are alleviated almost instantly. The cure is usually gradual "as the faith comes." When relieved and sufferers thank him (for he never takes money,) he says to them all: "Don't thank me; thank the Heavenly Father. Put your faith in Him, not in me. I have no power but what He gives me through my faith. He will give you the same."

There is no clap-trap, no affectation of mystery, no effort for notoriety in the man's doings. A gangway has been erected so that but one person can approach him at a time. He comes out, and, standing at one end of this gangway, in full sight of the crowd, receives each one passing through, and, without asking questions, seizes the individual's hands in his own crossed hands for a longer or shorter period, nearly always closing his eyes or raising them aloft and muttering a brief, silent supplication for Divine Grace. He stands there hatless and without a coat six hours every day, treating the afflicted. Some come day after day and stand in the crowd in the street before they are able to reach him. Often by daylight there is a crowd in front of the cottage in North Denver, a suburb of the city, where he is the guest of a man whom he cured of deafness before he came to Denver. Before dismissing the multitude each morning and afternoon, he goes down among the carriages and treats the afflicted who have been thus brought to him, and who are unable to approach him by the gangway. His manner is serene and sympathetic and he affects no oddity whatever, save that he wears his abundant hair parted woman-fashion and falling in long curls upon his shoulders. This gives to his face in repose (but only in repose) a striking resemblance to many of the favorite pictures of Christ. This probably affects the imagination of many. The crowds that stand about all day — seldom less than from 1,200 to 1,500 at a time — are all earnest, even those who are curious are earnestly curious — and as reverential as at a church assembly. It is a solemn, beautiful, impressive scene, to which the noble glories of the great Rocky Mountain range, visible in the near perspective, form a fitting background. There is a simple majesty in the whole effect, full of a divine pathos. It takes a grasp upon the imagination. It stirs the springs of all generous and ingenuous feeling. Many weep. Fathers come with crippled children in their arms, mothers with pining sickly babes upon their breasts. The sympathizing people part to the right and left to give them place. You see the flush of doubting hope upon their faces as they advance, the throat swelling with choking emotion, the tears repressed in anxious eyes — ah, if this might in deed be the dear Christ who said, "Suffer little children to come unto me."

But no, this is not the Divine One, who wrought his kingly mercies by the resistless Word. This is but a poor, simple, unselfish brother, who has gained some small and incomplete measure of the Divine Power by surrendering himself utterly to the Holy Will.

The forty-days fast of Jesus is, I believe, still counted by the Christian church a miracle. Well, such miracle as that was, this poor brother has performed in the simplest and most unostentatious way, as effectually, and under more difficulties, than those which beset the Christ. There is, of course, plenty of room in this case, as in that of Jesus, for a scientific doubt, if the physical possibility were now an open question, which it is not. All the world knows it has been done many times. The remarkable thing about this man's fast was that he continued his ministry of healing throughout the whole period, at first walking and riding about from village to village in the valley of the Rio Grande, in New Mexico, and, during the latter part, at the residence, in the city of Albuquerque, of Mr. J. A. Summers, deputy clerk of the probate court, a family of good intelligence and eminent respectability.

I happened at Albuquerque on the last day of his fast, and I spent the concluding hours of the trial with him, holding his hands while he gave me an account of his life, and the events that had determined him to endeavor for the Christ-life. I remained with him till he sat down to the meal prepared for him. The brief and only half-audible prayer he offered, standing at the table with eyes uplifted before sitting down, was absolutely the noblest dramatic effect I have ever beheld — simplicity, solemnity and grandeur.

But, since this remarkable fast was not scientifically observed, nothing would be gained by going into details. Space does not permit me to state the grounds of my faith in its perfect genuineness. The scene was inexpressibly moving and the last moments were ones of compassionating anxiety to all of us who were permitted to remain with him. We felt, of course, that there was danger in this eating a substantial meal at once. I essayed to utter a caution "Have no fear." he said. "Have faith. The Father has sustained me through forty days, and this is His will."

The table was beautifully laid for him alone, friends having brought flowers which were spread about on the immaculate, polished linen. The meal was a substantial one. Of the dozen or so who stood about, perhaps all feared the result, but I was the one of least faith. I was so sure that it would kill him that I could not remain. I said to myself, "He is now tackling a purely physical proposition — the rest of it has been largely psychical — he will be a dead man in six hours or less."

That was at 5 in the afternoon. He ate very heartily of fried chicken, beefsteak, and fried eggs, served with a bottle of good wine. Before retiring that night he ate another meal of bread and milk and, I understand, suffered no inconvenience from an act that would probably have killed nine hundred and ninety-nine out of any thousand men.

If the fast was genuine — and I do not myself doubt it in the slightest — the digestion of that meal was the closest approximation to a miracle of anything I have ever known. It demonstrates that what we call a purely physical proposition may have sometimes a large, if incommensurable, relation with the Spiritual.

The man has not sought notoriety. It has been thrust upon him. He does nothing in a sensational way, but is modest and meek in all. He does not proclaim himself Christ from the house-top, but when asked, he quietly but firmly says, "I am." He answered thus to me when I held his hand during the last moments of his fast.

The papers of Denver and Albuquerque have generally treated his mission with perfect candor, and the excitement has required them to devote from two to four or five columns a day to the case.

I close with a brief chronology of his life taken from his own lips.

Name, Francis Schlatter; born April 29, 1856, at Ebersheim, canton of Chlastad, Alsace, France; parents poor people who tilled some soil and spun and wove some coarse fabrics; parents dead; one brother and two sisters living in Alsace; never went to school after fourteen; learned the trade of shoemaking; has never married; came to America in 1884; spent several years in New York and at Jamesport, Long Island, working at his trade, interspersed with firing on steamboats in the local waters; came to Denver in the fall of 1892, and remained till next July, when he "had to" go forth on a mission of self-denial and healing; began to contemplate the Christ-life first in Denver, but realizes now that "The Father" had guided him specially for the previous five years, but not till then conscious of the guidance; born and reared a Catholic and is a Catholic still; as a baby of one year of age, was blind, deaf and raptured; has always been a little hard of hearing till he cured himself by faith in "The Father;" "had to" go forth from Denver afoot; arrested at Hot Springs, Ark., as a lunatic, because found barefooted and bare-headed, and claiming to be guided by "The Father;" was kept five months in jail; when first put in, the prisoners tried him in "The Kangaroo Court" (a common proceeding) and levied a fine, which not being able to pay, he "had to" take fifty lashes on his bare back; after that the prisoners treated him kindly and he healed many of them; liberated May 14, 1893, and went to Texas, where he was again put in jail at Throckmorton for one day as a lunatic; then "had to" tramp to California slowly, healing as he went; very successful among the Mexican villages, especially with little children and infants, but no so successful with grown people as now; followed generally the line of the Southern Pacific and El Paso westward, but could not ride, "had to" walk; fasted by spells voluntarily, many days at a time; went by steamer from San Diego up to San Francisco; "had to" go by steamer; December, 1894, was in San Francisco and did some healing; "had to" leave there on foot and tramp southward to Mojave; from there "had to" strike eastward across the great Mojave desert (the greatest and completest desert in North America) following the line of the Atlantic & Pacific railroad, at the stations of which he was allowed to fill his canteen with water; had nothing but flour and water and was barefooted; in March, 1895, reached Flagstaff, Ariz., where he "had to" go to herding sheep "to become a shepherd" for a while; leaving there, came eastward to Fort Wingate, N.M., and went up among the Navajo Indians healing, living five days with the Chief; then struck for the Rio

Grande valley which he reached in July at La Lunas: began his forty days' fast July 6, 1895, before reaching Las Lunas; fast ended August 15, at Albuquerque; has always been a laborious man up to the time he was "called" at Denver to go forth as a healer; first discovered his power to heal by curing a friend far away by letter.

This, in brief, is the history of a man whom as high as 5,000 people in a single day have crowded to see and be touched by in Denver. How miserable and contemptible a history it will seem to thousands, who think the history of John the Baptist, living on locusts and wild honey, with but a mean girdle about his loins, glorious!

Let us remember that it is we who think Saint John's life of self-surrended glorious. The greater part of his contemporaries — all the prosperous and proud who were interested in preserving the status quo — thought him a contemptible and vicious lunatic, and they cut his head off to stop the wagging of his trenchant tongue!

I consider the candor, the interest and the sympathy with which this poor, simple Alsatian has been received in Denver, where his history is known, as one of the most remarkable and thought-compelling events I have ever witnessed. The Rev. Myron Reed, the most noted pulpit orator of the West, preached a strong and sympathetic sermon on the man's character and mission recently, in which he said: "We have in our midst today a man whose credentials are as good as those possessed by Jesus of Nazareth before, and when he marched to the Jordan to be baptized by John.

"He has helped me morally.

"He is doing good here. He is calling our attention to the fact that the center and source of all life is God. Not a God who, a long time ago, filled a cistern and then went away; but God, a free-flowing spring, a present help in every time of need."

FITZ MAC.

CHAPTER III.

THE HEALER IN DENVER.

In fulfillment of his promise to E. L. Fox, Esq., the Healer left Albuquerque for Denver by train on the 21st of August, 1895. The press of Colorado had kept the public advised of his remarkable fast of forty days at Albuquerque and his successful healing and unceasing work during its continuance. When it became certain that he would go to Denver for public work the interest was remarkably intense, not alone in Colorado, but in all the adjoining states, extending even to the Pacific coast and largely overspreading the Eastern states. "The Healer is coming," went with the speed of lightning along his route, and this was enough to attract thousands who were anxious to touch his hand or have him bless handkerchiefs for their healing. In many cases the conductor was constrained to hold his train to the farthest limit to gratify the popular demand to even see the wonderful man. At every station the sleeper he occupied was instantly besieged by the eager throng, so that is was impossible for him to get the rest he so badly needed after his exhausting experiences at Albuquerque. To the sick and suffering his very presence was a blessing and his divine touch made them whole. No potentate could have been more honored than he on that memorable journey, and surely none would have left so many grateful hearts in his wake.

By an unavoidable delay in his train he was missed by his friend, Mr. Fox, who had been awaiting his arrival in Denver, and he sought rest at the nearest public house. Even at the midnight hour the news that the Healer had arrived rapidly spread and crowds soon congregated around his hotel — some moved by a morbid curiosity and others hoping his magic touch might give them health and new life. But they were disappointed, for Mr. Fox, at 6 a.m., took him in a closed carriage to a retreat provided for him in North

Denver, where he could have the quiet he needed to recuperate from his phenomenal and exhausting labors. Here a singular phase of human nature was witnessed. It was well known by the public that the Healer needed and demanded rest — that he was physically exhausted — and that he had promised to commence his public healing as soon as he was fitted for the task. But the curiosity of the rabble was brazen and impudent, while the importunity of the afflicted was pitiable. The one was barbarous in its disregard of the proprieties, while the attitude of the other said, "Give, give," no matter at what cost to the Healer. To shield him from this clamorous and indecent disregard of his sacred right to rest and quiet, it became the daily and hourly duty of those whose gratitude offered him this asylum to warn presumptuous intruders from the premises until he had recovered his strength.

After two weeks of such experiences he became the guest of Mr. Fox, whose cottage in North Denver is regarded as a Mecca and revered as sacred because this Divine Man here gave the world a needed lesson in practical Christianity and reenacted the works of the Galilean Master. Here his Denver work opened and here it continued until his mysterious exodus on the night of November 13th, 1895.

On the minds of the many thousands who here beheld him perhaps no scene has been so graphically and indelibly impressed as that which daily occurred in front of the Fox cottage. The power of speech to describe this is lame and impotent. It is easy to state that multitudes came and went. That could be said of any kind of a crowd, drawn together by any kind of an impulse. But it is not so easy to give expression in words to that subtle something that shone through the countenance and was dimly seen by the physical eye. Every face in that vast multitude was a study. Idle curiosity had been displaced by sincere and searching inquiry. Here was something that arrested attention and was worth investigation. Here seemed an answer to the universal prayer and expectation that somehow, somewhere, would be found a short cut to health and happiness. That this desire is well nigh universal but few will deny, and it was but an easy step to see in the Healer its fulfillment. It was not alone the Healer, nor the line of waiting, patient, hopeful invalids, nor the throng that filled the streets by the thousand that made the picture as one would paint or photograph a landscape. It was a composite with the Divine Man in a setting of the faces, forms, attitudes, expressions and all that the human soul can show itself to be when looking through the "human face divine." Faith, hope, awe, reverence, were as plainly apparent on the faces of the

multitude as if each had been separately labeled. To each one seemed to come out of the dim past a faint remembrance, a bringing forward into actuality that which had hitherto been a hope or a dream.
Here it was easy to recall the incidents in the public ministry of the
Man of Sorrow, as yet unapproached in the annals of time. At the
distance of more than nineteen centuries we can look though the
mists of the intervening ages and see the great heart, the infinite
love, the unselfish compassion of One who was wholly moved by a
desire to aid His fellows without a thought of personal reward.
From sea, shore, lake and mountain we can recall the scenes surrounding the Master — His faithful followers, the multitudes, the
maimed, the halt, the blind, the sorrowful — and see His uplifted
hands in healing and benediction. His attitude, His personality, His
works were unique. Nothing cared He for synagogue, doctor, priest
or the established order. His one impulse was to be about the
business of the Father. To listen to the Divine Voice and follow
where it led, without question, was His mission.

From that scene to this, by the mysterious processes of mental
photogravure, was but a step. Here before our eyes was presented
the similitude of all we have read or imagined of the earthly work of
the Master of Galilee. True, he did not raise the dead, literally, but
he raised the diseased and suffering from sickness and pain to an
estate of health and happiness. In all essential particulars here was
the startling proof of the words of Jesus, "He that believeth on Me
the works that I do shall he do also." Not alone were the benefits
conferred upon the bodies of the people, but upon their minds and
souls. Hundreds carried their Bibles with them, and it was not un-
common to see groups examining the Scriptures for proofs of this
divine method of healing. To many minds the lesson was deep and
abiding. The atheist and materialist were here confronted with a
stupendous Fact, which was more to them than all theological
speculations or mountains of creeds and dogmas. From indif-
ference and acutal skepticism many were aroused to a deep interest
in things unseen and carried away with them an awakened hope
that the claims of sacerdotalism were not all a sham.

At his appointed place, in sun or storm, and with uncovered
head, for six hours each day, in obedience to the Voice of the Father
and by His mighty power, this modern man of sorrow and agony
ministered unto the sick and afflicted and healed their hurts. The
fame of this service rapidly increased the throng until it became so
great that willing hands lent help to bring order out of confusion by
registering and placing in line all who wished to touch his hand.
Without this precaution inextricable confusion must have been the

result. His work commenced at 9 a.m., but many hours before that time a line was formed, from two to four abreast, extending sometimes around three sides of a large square. At noon he took a recess of one hour, when he resumed and closed his public work for the day at 4 o'clock. Often hundreds in line failed to reached him at that hour. But their patience and hope were sublime, and not infrequently many of these retained their places all the following night in order to be sure of treatment next day. No inclemency of weather deterred those anxious and persistent souls from their purpose. At 3 a.m. and sometimes sooner, the people commenced to arrive and take their places, and by the time the Healer made his appearance a vast multitude was waiting in line, and the street in front of where he stood was thronged by thousands. On the latter, who were mostly curiosity seekers, his very presence seemed to cast a feeling of awe and involuntary respect. No police supervision was necessary, though the multitude often numbered over five thousand. No confusion or disorder, no boisterous talking, but good humor, hopefulness, and voices hushed to the lowest and most respectful tones. They acted as though in a divine presence and were standing on holy ground.

As the Healer stood there and blessed the afflicted with his touch as they rapidly passed before him, telling each one to "thank the Father;" with a countenance whereon peace and an abiding faith were expressed; with a directness of purpose and self-poise denoting a full realization and understanding of his work and its lesson; with clear blue eyes, which shone with a love that was universal in its reach; with lips silently uttering the Lord's prayer, and with a face that filled our highest ideal of the face of Jesus, the conviction was overpowering that mortals were again standing face to face with the Divine Master. Here, also, was one who had no regard for the institutions or customs of men and was not moved by the impulses common to the race. No thought of fruits of his labors and sufferings ever entered his mind. He abhorred the idea of receiving compensation. Even the Nazarene could not have been more free from the moving motives of the unbelieving rabble in the streets of Jerusalem. And it was this, more than all else, that made him a wonder and a mystery to doctor, priest, preacher, and to all the shades and degrees of people who are ingrained with the blighting greed of our spurious civilization. They could not see beneath the surface of this lowly and godly man and read the secret of his heart. Why he should, from day to day, from week to week, from month to month — until his ministry in Denver covered eighty days — give the fruits of his divine gift "without money and without price," was incomprehensible to the average mind. If his object had been worldly gain it could have been easily gratified, for many thousands of dollars were either actually tendered to him or only awaited the assurance that they would be accepted when offered. "No, Father says no," was his uniform reply to all offers of compensation. To all who can see, his work was a lesson and a *warning* to the prevailing greed and venality, and to check, in a measure at least, "man's inhumanity to man." But it had a deeper meaning and conveyed a broader lesson, which can be understood alone in the light of his prophetic visions. To "the damnable dollar" — as he tersely interpreted the phrase, "the love of money is the root of all evil" — can be justly charged all the monumental crimes against humanity, and his righteous indignation against this barbarism knew no bounds. It was plain to him, as it is to all humanitarians, that greed is the curse of the age; and both his intuition and the voice of the Father taught him that we can have no justice on earth while we have institutions and forms of government in which the "damnable dollar" is a prime factor, for these are but hotbeds for the forcing of this "giant weed." Therefore his great lesson to the world in his Denver ministry was that man owes a higher duty to both God and man than the robbery and spoilation of his fellows, and that no tinkering with the prevailing forms of government can in any wise eradicate this evil from them, but that they must be wiped from the face of the earth to give place to the Divine Order in human affairs so plainly foreshadowed by the Word of God and the Infinite Evolutionary Stress. No wonder a greedy, godless and materialistic world could not understand this. But it will soon be forced to comprehend the full meaning of the lesson. In the view of the Healer, no less than in the view of thousands of awakened souls, we are on the eye of such momentous throes as this earth has not yet experienced. Not forever can we be indifferent to the Infinite Decree to discard the worn-out and effete and accept something better. The "better way" was here dimly foreshadowed, for on the memory of the thousands who were eye-witness of this marvelous scene, perhaps no more enduring impression was made than the broad and deep and Divine Love of one who forgot self and all personal rewards in his humble and beneficent ministry to the sick and suffering.

With him rank, wealth and position were as baubles. Side by side in the line were the most cultured and the most illiterate; the rich, clad in fine raiment, and the poor, in rags and patches. To him all were alike, all the children of one Father, and all receive his tender ministrations. He did not know if he held the hand of the millionaire or that of the beggar; the child of fortune and luxury or the child of sin and shame and sorrow. A love free from condemnation and a charity that was boundless were expressed in every look and act. He did not even say, as the Master did to one who had received His divine touch, "Go and sin no more," but let the healing potency flow through him to all alike. The terrible ordeal through which he had passed in order to develop this divine gift had been forgotten in this present fulfillment of his mission.

To look at the expectant multitude one would think that all the world was sick. From near and far had been brought maladies incurable by the medical profession. This, to them, was their last and only hope. The leprosy healed by Jesus was no more the despair of the "regulars" of Judea than were the diseases brought to the Healer. Yet hope and expectation could be seen on every face that he would set them free from their burdens. In many, many cases this hope became a reality. Of the eighty-seven thousand who received his touch at that memorable spot, thousands were healed. If it should be asked why all were not so fortunate, it may be answered, as it was stated of the Master on a certain occasion, that "he did not many mighty works because of their unbelief." No doubt each weary heart in that pathetic line and hope and expectation, but not every one had the abiding, unshaken faith. Without this not even the power of God could heal them. If this was true of Jesus, the same law held good with the Healer. But the astounding fact remains that very many were healed. In this volume no specific cases of healing are given, because to give these would unduly increase its size. To give all — if that were possible — or any considerable percentage of them, in the hope of convincing the unbeliever or the scoffer, would be wasted effort. These would not believe though hundreds were raised from the dead. By an illustrious example we are warned against casting "pearls before swine." It is enough to say that from the grateful hearts of thousands that were healed ascend daily prayers for the welfare and safety of the Healer, whose memory is revered as one divinely appointed to perform the Master's work. Whatever his farther mission on earth may be, whatever his present whereabouts of condition, what farther trails and hardships may be put upon him by the Father, or when he may make his next advent among men to perform the works yet reserved for him, certain it is that a stream of love and gratitude goes out from multitudes whose hearts and homes are open to receive him whenever it shall please the Father to call him back.

On the last day he treated over 5,000. Fully as many awaited the morrow's blessing, but alas for them, it never came. On the morning of November 14, 1895, the Fox household found the Healer's room vacant. On the pillow was found this:

"Denver, November 13, 1895.

"Mr. Fox — My mission is finished. Father takes me away. Good-bye."

(Signed)   "FRANCIS SCHLATTER."

This discovery caused something like the grief of Mary at the tomb of her arisen Lord to load the hearts of his faithful friends in the Fox family — a grief that found vent in tears and lamentations. These knew him best of all, at that time, because their intimate associations with him had given them the best opportunity. Whatever the world might think, here were those who knew, not alone his power, but the purity of his life and his marvelous love and unselfishness.

Outside of that cottage a memorable scene was being enacted. The excitement, the disappointment and, in some cases, the insane rage and unjust accusations of those who had expected to be blessed by his touch that morning, when told of his mysterious disappearance, are simply indescribable. A few cursed and swore, many shed disconsolate tears, while a gloom like the pall of death and hopelessness fell upon the mass, who silently and with heavy hearts marched again and again around the square that had been the scene of his labors, content to take away some souvenir of the Healer, if but a splinter from the fence in front of the Fox cottage or a handful of earth on which his feet had stood. A great light and hope had been taken out of their lives. And this was true also of the greater multitudes en route, coming almost by the train loads from all points of the compass. So genuine and so far-reaching a sorrow has rarely fallen to the lot of any historian to record. But the Healer was gone and if any one knew where, or how he went, his purpose or his destination, the public was not advised of it. Where had been life, animation, glad hope and that mysterious figure in their midst at his labor of love, now was desolation.

Though the Healer, as far as the privileges of citizenship are concerned, had the undoubted right to go when and where he pleased, yet as soon as it was known that he was gone, detectives and reporters, with indecent haste, and, apparently, to achieve small notoriety for themselves, rushed over the country lik a pack of bloodhounds on the trail of a fugitive from justice. Just what they would have done with him if they had found him it would have been hard for even themselves to have told. In their unworthy zeal they did not hesitate to invade the privacy of the most retired homes and to prowl at night, with "strong night glasses," peering through the windows of private residences at all hours of the night. In the history of so-called journalism, and the prying indecency of detective work, it would be rare to find a parallel to his unmanly search for one who had committed no crime, and whose only notoriety was found in that fact that he had arisen on the horizon of a materialistic and venal world unheralded by earthly methods and, in his beneficent work, was a marvelous rebuke to the greedy scramble for "that damnable dollar." The press and the wires of the telegraph were kept busy in heralding deceptive reports that he had been found first here and then, there until at last he had been certainly located at a private and unpretentious home hear Boulder. But this mysteriously eluded their most vigilant search. How he did this is as inexplicable as the power by which he healed the sick. But he did it; and alone, without money or human aid, he successfully made the trip of nearly a thousand miles during the most inclement weather of the winter, to the retreat to which the Father had directed him at Hermosillo ranch in the mountains of southwestern New Mexico. In this desolate journey, with it perils, its inevitable incident of hardships and dangers and a portion of it which, to human view, would have been fatal to the most hardy and expert frontiersman, is to be found the greatest proof of his divine guidance and providential aid.

In his room when he left the Fox cottage it is said were over fifty thousand unanswered letters containing handkerchiefs for his blessing. Up to the time of his departure he had devoted all his leisure hours to his mail, but no single human being could keep pace with the flood that daily reached him. In the history of the postal service this instance stands without an equal. No presidental candidate — either before or after election — ever received the same number of letters in the same time, and they came from every state in the Union and from nearly all foreign lands. They were not alone from the illiterate and superstitious but mainly from the cultured and educated. These had sought relief from all human means and failed. But "the heart of things" had opened their eyes to the fact that deeper than in material helps was to be found their healing. And it is remarkable that with the multitudinous doctors and drugs now spread all over the earth the thought is taking shape and spreading that no permanent good can come from these, but that true healing must come from the source of All Life, and that it is but impeded by materialistic means.

It may safely be stated that since the days of the prophets of old no one has suffered so great hardships, exposure, perils and personal torture by a divine leading for spiritual unfoldment as the

Healer. No explanation of this experience is here attempted. It was a matter between the Healer and his God. That he was loyal to the Voice that guided him and true to the Divine Purpose — at whatever cost to his personality — is the one amazing incident in such an age as this. That he firmly believes he has a mission for the uplift of the race is well attested by what he has already done; and that he will follow his Divine Voice to its final accomplishment those who know him best do not have a doubt. Fidelity to what he believes to be his duty will lead him to endure future hardships and perils though it should finally land him at the stake.

Such scenes as those attending his healing ministry have not been enacted since the Son of Mary, with infinite love, took compassion on the suffering multitudes of Judea. To the world at large the man and his mission are meaningless mysteries, but no more so than were the life and works of Jesus. One was misunderstood, maligned, persecuted and crucified, because He obeyed the Father and disregarded the established order of human affairs. What He endured from the age of twelve to the date of His public ministry, in order to prepare Himself for that work, the world may never know. The history of the eighteen years of His life of which we have no record must be read in the light of intuition alone. That they were devoted to preparation for the work of His Father must be admitted by all thoughtful minds. No other view will furnish an adequate explanation of that marvelous life.

This modern type of the Master has also suffered in his preparation — has borne imprisonment and stripes, has suffered in hunger, exposure and voluntary fasting, and is as much misunderstood — but it is late in the day for another Calvary. The superhuman powers of the One were the credentials He offered to an unbelieving race as a testimony of His devine mission. The story of the One was written with loving faithfulness by His disciples as a lesson, a testimony and a warning to mankind. The other is his own biographer and by his own hand has written the story of his life, his journeyings, his sufferings in order to make him the fit instrument of the Father. By his own hand and also through an amanuensis, he wrote his prophetic visions as *another and a last warning* from the Almighty and a command to "come up higher." That this command must be obeyed — at whatever cost to present human institutions — is as sure as that God lives. Disobedience will bring disaster in the present and the future, as it has always in the past. "Obey or be crushed" has come thundering down the ages, and the tones of that Omnipotent Voice are now ringing in the ears of mankind. Let the prophecies of the Healer interpret its meaning.

JOSEPH WOLFF.

CHAPTER IV.

TEACHINGS IN RETIREMENT.

A January night at 8,000 feet elevation means intense cold. If you are a traveler in the Datil Range, it brings extreme suffering. Physical nature is not kind here. Indoors, blazing pitch-pine knots defy outdoor cruelty, and invite to back log studies the hours of peaceful meditation.

Karl was learning English, and could reach rapidly Henry Wood's "Ideal Suggestion." The large lettered Idealism was imparting a double lesson, having a charm for us both, when doors suddenly opened and closed.

"Hill has probably forgotten to take the morral off his horse," with quaint comment, said the keen western juvenile.

"Yes," I answered, "he forgot last night. Poor thing! I'm glad he has gone over to the barn to take it off. It's a bleak, cold night for a horse to stand out, tied up, and with a morral on that!"

Distant doors opened and closed. I was holding the book high, at arm's length. Karl was reading, as the leaves turned, "I am Soul." "I am Free." "Pain is Friendly." "God is Here," when unexpectedly the parlor door sprung open. Turning and peering into the hall, we saw, famed by the dark doorway, "The Silent Man of Denver" — the same strange looks, the uncovered head, the long, waving hair, the gentle attitude, the peaceful face, with all those impressive characteristics that thousands saw and can never forget. We rose instantly, motionless, gazing out into the dimly-lighted hall. The humble Alsatian stood silent, quietly waiting, but I could not move and dared not speak. It was the supreme moment of my life. Is this chance? If not, there is a God, and He is Good. Is this accident? If not, fear is dead, and I see a greater death. It is not even now too late. Instantly the truth of the merciful law of compensation was made Manifest. The sorrowful past was glorified. Unalloyed joy filled my being. For the first time the Great Unseen had heard and answered prayer when offered. Again, like a tidal wave, the memory of the Via Dolorosa swept over the soul, but I knew inwardly it was finished. Intuitively I saw a vast and happier future and knew I was free. Wondering at this stupendous event that caused me such astonishment, the mysterious visitor broke the long, silent strain, saying, "Good evening," in a full, low voice.

The awful thought-pressure thus relieved by his words, I fell from ecstatic heights. By leaps and bounds I reached and grasped the extended hand and silently led him to a rocking chair beside the brilliant open fire, feeling as Paul must have felt when he saw the light that stunned him on the way to Damascus. After piling on more wood, as he sat by the broad fireplace, we stood looking steadily at him to be fully convinced that it was no optical illusion. I asked:

"Aren't you cold?"

"Not very," he replied simply.

"When did you come?"

Glancing at the clock he replied, "Maybe three-quarters of an hours ago. I came over and knocked, but no answer. So I went back to the barn and fed my horse, for Father told me it was a house of faithfuls. Then made down my bed. Then I saw a light and came back again and knocked several times, but again no answer. Then I crossed the canyon, saying to myself, 'They will see me in the morning,' I was preparing to go to sleep when the horses moved about. Throwing back the blanket, I sat up and saw a man standing looking at me, and he said, 'Hello; why didn't you come over to the house?' I told him I had made two trips, both unsuccessful, when he invited me to come with him. And I am here."

Recalling the pledge made to my higher self last fall in Denver, I said:

"Karl, who is that?"

"The Healer of Denver," he answered instantly, pointing to the mantel shelf, "I know him by his picture."

Then I realized the situation and saw defeat. Having, by this time, recovered sufficiently from the shock to think clearly, I asked his future intentions and what was his desire, and if he wished his arrival made known.

"Father says no," looking up and away in that habitual listening attitude. "When they find it out Father says I must go."

I understood the spirit of "See thou tell no man," and in five minutes we were all solemnly pledged to secrecy, and no word escaped us that marvelous winter.

Laboring under the confusing consciousness of the possibilities of such a visit, meanwhile giving silent unfeigned praise and thanksgiving, the duties of hostess suddenly dragged me from those mystic regions of imagination; remembering, too, that he was flesh, with belated hospitality I asked:

"When have you had food?"

"Not much for days, but at noon with a Mexican sheep-herder, who did not recognize me, I took some coffee and beans."

"Where, did you say?"

"Over there, twenty miles from here," pointing northwest.

"When were you in Albuquerque?"

"I've not been there."

"Well! Then you saw the engineer, Norris, as you crossed the A. & P. railroad?"

"No."

"You must have seen the men who had my letter to Mrs. Summers inviting you to rest here?"

"No."

"Then you certainly inquired for this ranch as you traveled south?"

He laughed his first hearty, jovial, long peal as I persisted in tracing his arrival to material means or methods, saying:

"No! How could I inquire for something I did not know existed? Father wanted me here, so He brought me. There is a work for me to do here, otherwise I would not have been directed to this place. If your house had been in a yawning hold at the top of a hill, when I reached that hill Father would say, 'Go up there.' Should I murmur, as I often do, asking 'Why? What for?" like always, He would say, 'Because I want you to go up there.' I had to find this house," with continued laughter, as he saw the unsatisfied look at his unusual explanation. Travelers commonly rely upon people or sign boards, telegrams or other earthly means of communication.

"Well, now that you are here, I should like to have you stay till the Fourth of July, or a year, or as long as you please," thinking of where I saw him three months before, with miles of misery, degenerates, the physically defective, passing before him. This invitation brought forth another long, loud, merry shout of laughter as he shook his head, saying:

"O, no. Not that long. But Father promised me a long rest in southwestern New Mexico, when I was lying in that barn in Colorado for three days and nights without food or water, during the snowstorm last November. He said, 'I have prepared a place for you.' Then this afternoon, as I complained, He said, 'Keep on going.

You are coming to a ranch.' 'But,' I said, 'suppose they don't invite me to stay and rest?'' 'Well, if they don't you must leave early in the morning; but they know you; they will invite you.''' Which doubtless caused the laugh of contentment when I spoke as I did.

The other rooms being freezing cold, a small dining table was placed in front of his easy chair, and as I came and went, preparing his meal, I noticed he looked contantly at the book shelves when not answering the fusilade of questions about his remarkable trip, on one horse, in the dead of winter, from Denver to Datil. When all that the ranch had to offer was prepared and set before him, I knew it had been long delayed and apologetically said:

"You must be half starved."

Meekly he said, "I can eat; but I've been days without food since I left Denver." There by the open, cheerful, crackling fire, how free, genial and happy he was! Indoors at last, out of the bleak, dreary, vast waste of the snow and rocks! Stange man! Refusing all money, declining the special trains put at his service, ignoring worldy honors and attentions, quietly mounting the beautiful white horse, he rode away from the field of his ministrations in Colorado and traveled due south 700 miles or more, and stole in upon us "like a thief in the night," unannounced, unlooked for!

He recounted, as he slowly ate, the details of his journey to us, being seven weeks and six days en route, having left Denver on the night of November 13th, 1895, without money, and thereafter rarely having food or even shelter. To us however, the account of his journey after crossing the Atlantic & Pacific railroad was especially interesting. Alone on the massive Putney Mesa, covered with snow — how had he endured the ordeal? Slept there without fire, shelter or food! Reached Sebolleta after a perilous descent on this side, following an abandoned Indian trail, and there rested over Sunday. Thence due southeast.

I repeatedly broke in upon his detailed description of his dangerous trip with the constantly recurring question, "But how did you happen to find this one particular ranch, hid in a boxed-up canyon, as it were, out of the world? And you asked no questions or directions? No house for sixty miles the way you came! Had you followed the Rio Grande down, I could see; meantime knowing exactly where you were going. But thought that trackless, vast, undulating sea of cedar-covered earth-waves! The endless monotony! No landmarks; no water, for the Indians have covered up the springs. Then through gaps, passes, cut-offs and cow trails — those grama-covered draws, every one just like the others — why, it would take a Navajo Indian to pilot one across for the first time! A party of us went over there Christmas, hunting Indian ruins. I could get lost every five miles. It's a dismal, wretched country. We agreed to set trees on fire to signal the lost or strayed when merely out of sight of camp. To me that trip was like drifting at sea. No clear-cut landmarks, no roads, yet of course we knew where we started from and where we thought we wanted to go. But with you it was different — alone, your first trip, an utter stranger in the country. Old timers can easily get lost in there — and you without a guide?"

"No, no; not without a guide," he remarked, so solemnly that it intensified the silence, "for when I came to long valley out there, about for or five miles from the house, I said to Father, 'Here is wood for fire, may I not camp?' 'No,' He said, 'keep on going. You are coming to the ranch.'"

In this way the hours passed, and long after midnight he was shown the room hastily prepared for him. Thus the most sublimely alone soul in creation entered our desolate home and became our honored guest. He who had overcome selfishness, who had No need but to follow where He leadeth, he who was conqueror, slept beneath our roof. Yet on dull, dead ears fell that omnipresent word, "Father!" "Father!"

That night, through all the remaining hours, one member of the household thought, living over the old battle ground, asking in mental torture, Is God principle or person? For years, in lonely soliloquy, had come the thought, Do you know the significance of that, to give up the personality of God? No mercy, no love, the falsity of the fatherhood idea? Atoms in human form are then nothing — no more than a spray of Niagara, played upon by a heartless force. It means blank pessimism; but it also means intelligence. According to Lecky, the world morally is no better for our inventions and modern standards. We know a little more, perhaps; but tested by righteousness, on the whole we are a low order of creation. All we can do, therefore, . . . is to go on until death relieves, afterwards reveals the truth, answers the Why of it all. That little of logic is better than delusion. God is law, inexorable, relentless law!

But the Healer's familiar use of "Father" brought back all the Christian orthodoxy of my childhood teachings, revived the forgotten Scripture texts that He noted the sparrow's fall, was always so near and close that the hairs of our heads are numbered — conceptions abandoned with the years gone by. On that night and many following, the restlessness lasted until dawn. The head turned, tossed and plowed the pillow, awaiting sunrise. Then again to begin the day's routine in order to forget the agony of the darkness! The right conception of God is the most vital thought, of the greatest import. The supplication to have the Healer come under my roof had been granted; but the disappointment of the teaching implied by that omnipresent word, "Father!" Every reply to questions began, "Father says" — his own individuality submerged in the Unseen Presence. He had come, but only to destroy an edifice built by thorough reading and long investigation. I had successfully thought out, almost fought out, the idea of a personal God. But the one whose life was beautiful, ideal and unselfish came only to tear down the cherished shrine where the soul had long and silently worshipped — self-taught, self-sufficient, self-satisfied!

While preparing breakfast we heard the words of the familiar hymn enlivening the quiet home life:

"To our bountiful Father above
We will offer the tribute of praise
For the glorious gift of His Love
And the blessings that hallow our days."

Repeatedly he sung it until the meal was ready. Knowing the value of absolute separation from humanity, the second meal was carried to his room, where he ate alone. After the meal he turned to the table and picked up the Bible, saying:

"Do you remember the twelfth chapter of Daniel?"

"No, I do not read the Bible any more," I replied.

"I will read to you this chapter," said he. If I had expressed my honest thought I would have said, "Worse and more of it!" We can get some light and comfort from the New Testament, but he has gone back to that ancient history which the higher criticism admits is uninspired, and much of it unauthentic!" Nevertheless he read clearly, with comments constantly interspersed on the application of that mystic book to our day and age. He would read, rise to his feet and pace the floor as the prophecy was explained, proving that the race had not lived or passed the period Daniel is said to describe. "The 'abomination of desolation' is yet to be set up," he vehemently affirmed. "Such frightful days are ahead of humanity as have never been upon the earth. It is Father's Will. He lets do. But He will show them His power before complete dismay and destruction overtake the seemingly hopeless cause of the masses against the infernal spirit of oppression brought down on the people by the rulers, the leaders. Those are the ones! The leaders have been untrue, and the people mourn. But we are coming to the end of that. A New Dispensation is approaching. We are in the dawn of the Reign of Justice. Humanity must have a chance, for it has outgrown present oppressions. They are all here, all here. But good will overcome evil finally, and then we shall have the Kingdom!"

So the hours flew by, freighted with strange teachings. When

dinner was prepared and taken to his room, he looked up pleasant-
ly, asking:

"Why do you serve my meals in the room alone?"

"Because I thought even such association with ordinary mortals
would interrupt the necessary quiet of your life. I thought you were
of the order of the Asiatic Adepts, and had to be alone as much as
possible," I answered.

"O, no. If you will, I prefer to eat with the family," he replied.

"We would be both honored and privileged, of course, but did not
think of such a thing."

From that hour he was as free as possible under the conditions of
strictest retirement from the world, and came and went with
perfect liberty, as if he were in his own home in France, though
some one always preceded him before he went over to the barn to
visit Butte several times daily. A glance up and down the canyon, as
a precaution, was habitual to his attendant, to save a sudden surprise and consequent public knowledge of his whereabouts. He was
a constant Bible reader, and no one can put into that esoteric
library of books more illumination, life and hope, than Francis
Schlatter. When not reading Daniel it was Ezekiel, but always the
idea of a daily application of liberty, love, and help for the better-
ment of man.

The number of days mentioned in the last chapter of Daniel he
treated as prophetic of his return and, therefore, must have accepted the literal interpretation of the same, reading it repeatedly
aloud or quietly alone. I looked forward to the days when the ac-
quaintance would justify freedom of discussion, holding that the
Sermon on the Mount would help the average soul more than
mystic prophecies. Those happy days came speedily.

About 2 o'clock we sent for Butte, and under the massive, tall
pine tree they stood. The Healer laid his right arm listlessly across
Butte's back and neither moved for half an hour. Horse and owner
seemed one in intimate friendship and close consciousness of the
deep purpose of the relationship. A truer, more affectionate or
responsive spirit never inhabited horse flesh. Butte's funny doings,
his quick coming down the mountain side when he heard the whis-
tle — the signal for hot mash — and, at the last, his faith in us,
shown by his seizing every opportunity to walk into the house when
a door was thoughtlessly left open, and the memory of his dining off
sugar, meanwhile upsetting the bowl before any one knew of such
expressions of confidence, will ever be cherished tenderly and help
to recall the happier phases of home life that winter.

The subject of cruelty to animals naturally and frequently came up for consideration, years on the frontier and living on the open cattle ranges of the southwest had brought bitterest experiences in the prevalent brutality toward the speechless world, and enable us to tell him horrible facts, indicative of custom and accepted methods. Unfortunately story writers uniformly omit those facts even from realistic novelettes of the western ranges. When the Orientals told us at the World's fair that they did not feel cordial toward our missionaries, and illustrated the idea by asking a man who was there in the capacity of a Christian to take up a stick and see what effect it would have on a dog, the animal, having never known a blow, moved not, hardly looking up. The full force of this story appealed to him so quickly that I felt secure in my heretical attitude toward so-called Christian nations on the one line of thought and conduct toward the animal world.

"Do you wonder," I asked, "that my prayer has been, since then, 'Orientalize our continent, Oh, Lord?'"

"No, I do not wonder, but I was not aware of the horrible thing you tell me of cruelty to cattle and horses. Especially I did not know what you meant by "docking' horses. It is a useless and dreadful custom, but in the Kingdom there will be only the natural. In the Kingdom, birds will be Nature's ornament, not that of a lady's bonnet."

"Oh! that reminds me," I said, "of the strange inconsistencies of some people. In Denver I attended a meeting of advanced thinkers, and a lady arose preaching 'all life is God's life,' while at the moment were tiny corpses of birds on her bonnet! I fell to meditation upon the measureless gap between words and deeds."

"I do not believe in cruelty," he commented, "but I was glad I had a quirt when Butte would not go down that abandoned Indian trail when we were coming down the Putney Mesa. It was narrow, steep and almost like steps on the face of the hill — and Butte balked. I got down and tried to lead him. But no, not a step. 'Well,' I said, 'you just will go down there, for there is no other way now. We can't turn and go back.' So I went behind with my quirt and he finally made up his mind to try it, it it did seem dangerous to look at.

That evening and many others were spent in listening to thrilling description of his long, two-years' walk. And the details he gave in conversation, which he positively refused to give later when told to write the events for publication, greatly intensifed the mysterious tale of agony and suffering.

After one of the first breakfasts taken with the family, as he sat beside the open hearth, his face was radiant as he exclaimed suddenly:

"Father says I can talk. He says this is the place where I can freely speak."

"What do you mean? You have always had the power of speech, haven't you? I queried.

"Ah! yes. But Father always told me to keep still before. Now I can talk!" and his face beamed with satisfaction.

To this strange permission can be traced the talks he gave on many questions. From cruelty to animals to the kindred topic of cruelty to children was the easiest step, and his mind was as clear and decisive on that as on other topics.

"The world must outgrow torturing the flesh of children in order to reach their mentalities. Bruising is a relic of barbarism," I suggested as a text.

"Well," he replied, "it was the best thing that ever happened to me as a six-year-old child. I didn't think the teacher was just to me. He whipped my hand for something. I never knew what mistake I had made. So I just concluded quietly never to go back; but I kept still about it. Mother dressed me every day and sent me to school, book in hand, but I persistently left the small village and played with bigger boys. I kept that going for weeks till that younger sister of mine caught me on the outskirts of the village and reported me immediately to my father, who punished me so severely that mother said I was blue as a violet from head to heels. But it was good for me. It taught me to go to school, and I did till after father's death, with one exception, where another teacher treated me unjustly and I again rebelled. But I did it defiantly that time."

"Tell me about your home life," I requested.

"My only brother is twenty years older than I. The two sisters are living, I suppose, though I have not written to them since my arrival in America. The married one I now see in black, as though mourning. She was the older and was always fond of me. It is a strange thing to some people, but do you know that for ten years at different periods she dreamed the same dream about me, and I know now it was a prophecy. I remember her face as she would say, 'I dreamed the same dream about you;' and no explanation was necessary, as we both came to expect it. It has four scenes, or parts, and I am now fulfilling them, though as a boy I laughed at her and made fun of her. No matter how I laughed, she would say, 'Francis, it has a meaning.' But to the dream:

"She saw me always alone; not the least like other young men. Always studying, thinking, quiet, but never associating with other young people. Next she saw me start to walk, and with such a sad, mournful face. Walk, walk, walk! All alone, sad and sorrowful,

"Next a curtain dropped. I was behind it and she tried to see, but no. No one could see behind the curtain. After a while the curtain was raised and I stood happy, smiling, though greatly changed, in the midst of an immense wheat field, surrounded by dancing, joyous children. The grain was ripe and waving. Oh! the beauty of the last scene! Every child was active, lovely and dancing from joy. Life itself was pure happiness for us all there. You see I am at present in the third act. The curtain is down. I've disappeared. No one may be permitted to peer behind the curtain, but in due season the curtain will rise, and I will then be in the wheat field and ready for the harvest — and the fourth part of my sister's dream will have been completed. According to Daniel I will return in 1899, probably, though with Father time is nothing. Don't you remember there are no dates in the Bible? Time is all one — time and eternity are the same to Father. But I am the happiest man in creation, for I know. During that long walk Father told me the glorious future for us all; the happy and peaceful days for the coming race — but not till after the troublous times."

Dinner time came and the meals were a positive nuisance as, with regular impertinence, the hours came to provide for the mortal man, when we were sitting at his feet listening to his glowing words, his joyous, detailed descriptions of life in France, and more particularly the minutiae of that horrible tramp and its mystic meaning to mankind.

If ceremonies have ever been helpful, the blessing at the table — the social shrine of the homelife — is to some the most beautiful; and I asked him if it had been his custom so to worship. Kindly came the reply, "As you wish."

Of course, he was invited to offer thanks and, in the same look and manner that ever characterized him, he said the Lord's Prayer. I observed that he had changed its meaning by the addition of a word and, in the evening, I called his attention to it by saying:

"Your rendering of the Lord's Prayer is not like the New Testament version."

"In what way do you mean?"

"You say, 'Thy will, *will* be done,' a powerful affirmation; and not the form of petition implied by the usual method taught with the use of that word only once." After some moments' silence he answered:

"If I say, 'Thy will, will be done' it is because Father taught me to say those words. I had forgotten the Lord's prayer during the long years of city life, of struggle and pain; but that is the truth. His will is to be done — Here and Now. We are living in Revelations. This dispensation is coming to a rapid close. Many read the Signs of the

Times and know that we are on the eve of a new order. But all is contained in the Lord's Prayer. I use no other form, for it is all there. Jesus said no other, taught no other — but they say and do not. Why don't they live those words?"

This daily sacrament is indelibly impressed upon the memory as one of the most beautiful and lasting of the many remarkable events of his home-life.

At the breakfast table he talked constantly and his words rang out loud and clear, and his gestures were free as any Frenchman's. He was telling of the Kindgom, and "enthusiasm" would be a mild word to describe his mental condition, for those who have not heard him talk can scarcely conceive the intensity of his language and emotions. I recall the event clearly, when a rustle made me start — not a noise exactly, merely the suggestion of a presence somewhere — and with a startled though whispered exclamation I jumped to my feet, saying, "H'sh!"

Closing the dining room door behind me I walked into the front hall, to find Mr. Swingle standing there with a conscious look of expectancy. I ushered him into the parlor, closing the doors. Rapidly and quietly leading the Healer to the other wing of the house, to the girls' room, I sat down to recover my equilibrium. Then I said deliberately:

"That is Mr. Swingle. He has ever been kind to us." With upraised hand he stopped me; the, listening as usual, presently said:

"Let him come in. Father says he can keep still," which made me laugh aloud, for it's a natural for Bill Swingle to keep all he knows to himself as for him to breathe. He never repeats what he must know is but current talk. In fact, he is exasperatingly secretive. It is almost a fault in him, for it is his policy, carried on with a vigilance none of us ever witnessed in another. With glee I went to the parlor and quizzed him about how long he had been standing in the hall and who and what he had heard. He answered as evasively as the occasion would allow, so I enlightened him by saying:

"Yes, you heard a man's voice; and true, it is that of a foreigner. Can you guess who it can possibly be?" I awaited a reply. As he did not deign to answer, I said, with unconcealed pleasure, "It's the Healer of Denver!"

How the weatherbeaten face shone! A deep flush tinted the bronzed skin; the eye lighted as he came to his feet trembling, and anxiously asked, "What?"

"True. It is indeed the very same. It was his voice you overheard, and he says you can see him — that you won't tell," at which we both laughed aloud, as his well-known characteristic had been discerned by the Healer before he ever saw or heard of him.

"Where's a comb? Just look at me! I can't go in this way."

"The idea!" I said. "Do you think he judges by appearances? He is too profound for that stupidity. Do you suppose he cares for externals? Come on."

So I led the way, introduced them and immediately retired. From that meeting Mr. Swingle had the entree of the house day and night, and was loyal and helpful. He kindly went to Magdalena more than once for provisions, and offered his services freely to aid in the entertainment of our Wonderful Guest during the happy winter of 1896.

The serious and perplexing phase, however, would come uppermost, with all the Healer's grasp of current questions, which he hourly evinced. Yet he evidently taught the anthropomorphic idea of God by the constant use of "Father says," "Father told me," this or that. Such terminology was inexplicable; yet Jesus laid claim to "the Father and I are one." Here is another in our age not only saying it but living it every hour. No one can be associated as were we and not see the close, sweet relationship of Father and Son, a nearness truly tender and beautiful. Yet such conscious sympathy is not vouchsafed to others, it would seem. We sit down determinedly to try to find out what was done nineteen centuries ago over the seas, while the only records have been changed and handled by the various peoples and councils. At the opportune time I must ask a few leading questions; for his complete retirement from the world gave every opportunity for seeking information; and no spirit was ever more broad and tolerant than Francis Schlatter's, as was amply proved and tested many times during those months of freedom at Hermosillo Ranch. When I questioned and doubted, he was gentle in his answers and clear in his opinions.

Still persisting in the refusal to read the Bible, as all oppressors and oppressions found authority for their conduct and ideas therein, yet by accident I changed suddenly when looking at his Bible one day. Because of the fact that Daniel's writings had fourteen chapters in his, I began to hunt about me for a Protestant translation and found Raymond's in the bookcase, one that had been used as a school text book. The idea of comparative studies fascinated me. His was a Catholic version, and to give the discrepancies we found would fill a book and would have little bearing on the life or teachings of this spiritualized individual on our earth today. When he found chapters left out, like the two of Daniel; when he compared them book by book and saw how much smaller the Protestant was than the Catholic, he showed as much surprise as at any time, saying sadly:

"The shepherds have troubled the waters; the sheep can get nothing of the pure truth to drink."

"Well, don't you think humanity ought, by this time, to be beyond the sheep symbol?" I queried.

"No!" he said decidedly. "Do you imagine man to be above leaders at this stage of evolution? Do you think mankind beyond teachers, rulers, governors? Not yet. I know the theory of the sovereignty of the individualist idea, but the world is not yet ready for that," he replied.

"But Jesus was the greatest individualist of history," I argued, "and His teachings ought to have lifted us beyond the sheep plane of development. Of course, if one sheep jumps they all do. Politically men may emulate their ways, but in religious life it would seem that we are all children of the One Infinite Power and Presence, and ought not to be dependent upon mimicking each other."

"You forget," said he, "that we, as a race, are in our infancy. Father often tells me that I am a mere youth of eighteen years, that I am only beginning to grow, and I shall develop wonderfully before I am brought back by Father when He needs me. I shall grow physically and spiritually also, while away from the world. It seems I must go away alone. No one will be permitted to go with me. Then, when He brings me back! Think of it! Jesus' teachings will be fulfilled. Then no more injustice, no more oppression, no more sin. We will have peace once and forever here on this earth."

"Why, that would be Heaven, my friend, and I thought you had to die to go to Heaven."

"No, no! Heaven can be here and now. Heaven is a condition, not a certain place. The Kingdom of Heaven is within, but the day cometh when the inward shall be the outward; when the Kingdom shall be actualized, be made manifest for the ripe fruit: the unripe will know better when they come back again."

His earnestness and eloquence knew no limitation when describing to me the incoming, joyous, new conditions and better order of the dawning dispensation.

"I can hardly wait in patience at times when I dwell on the beauty of this world-to-be. I wish it was all over and the establishment in progress today. But the day approaches, and I am the happiest man in creation," he would exclaim.

He certainly looked it. Undoubtedly he honestly felt it, and frankly gave invariable expression of faith in the Father's Purpose to fulfill the New Testament promises to the pure, good and meek. His good feeling and his sublime hope were contagious, and glimpses of the glory would overcome the doubts and dismal facts of present conditions. Humanity must come higher — but how? Judging by the past, only by the slow process of evolution and endless law of selection. Yet he would demur and say:

"You will see. It's coming quicker than you think. Father is going to take a hand in the affairs of men, and they will have cause to remember it for a long time!"

"Do you feel," I inquired, "that the New Testament is sufficiently clear on the incoming change which you prophesy, that no one need err, or mistake the time of the harvest?"

"Amply so; but Father says ninety-nine parts are left out by those who wrote of Jesus' sayings and doings. Yet the one part recorded contains enough truth to lead one upward and onward to the Eternal Light. Simply do the best you know how, and that alone in salvation. Go read the parable of the two sons. The one said he would not go to the vineyard; the other said he would, which was mere words, or a prayer. You see the first didn't pray, but went and did the work. His was action. Work is what Father wants. There has been too much talk for two thousand years. Now it's thought, action; thought, action; thought, action!"

As the midnight hours approached it occurred to me that here was one who combined the repose of the Oriental with the energy of the Occidental, was both a Pessimist and Optimist; an Iconoclast and Reconstructionist; Indifferent and Intense; Human and Divine; who came preaching that Illuminated Christianity is to be the natural religion of the future; that the Kingdom is at hand; that he has walked for the world; that his sufferings are the fire he went through for the world; that toward the close of the century there are to be no more words, it is deeds the Father demands; asks no help; is alone with the Father now, as he has been for years, and will be forever; that souls have now what they did before; that our work is our choice of good or evil. He says, "I have no material means. Father has all means and power, and by my faith I must prove to the world He can do all things. He has promised it to His children."

In substance he teaches that

" * * * One adequate support
For the calamities of mortal life
Exists, one only! — an assured belief
That the procession of our fate, howe'er
Sad or disturbed, is ordered by a Being
Of infinite benevolence and power,

Whose everlasting purposes embrace
All accidents, converting them to good."

II.

A February day brought Mr. Swingle back from his long journey
across the San Augustine Plains to Magdalena, the mountain
hamlet and only base of supplies for the surrounding country. The
Healer was sitting in the sunshine reading the Bible, when his
attention was suddenly arrested by some moving object down the
canyon, and simultaneously the suggestions was made that he
quickly get back into the house; meanwhile a closer inspection,
from the lookout point, proved the party to be only our trusted
friend bringing the needed provisions. As the freight wagon hove
into full view and the jaded, tired horses sighed as they stopped
beside the house, the Healer walked out to salute our friend and
helper, saying:

"Your have made good time. You left here early day before yester-
day. One hundred miles, round trip, in three days is steady work for
your horses, though not heavily loaded." Whereupon the conversation turned to the interesting incidents of camping out, the events
in the town, Butte's new shoes, and current topics generally.

By direct questioning one could not get a positive answer from
him as to any choice of food, or an expression of liking for any
particular article; always the same answer:

"I like anything you set before me. Food is not necessary to me
for many days at a time. Anything you happen to have I will eat
thankfully, but I have no choice."

However, I determined to decoy him into a description of his
mother's methods of cooking and, before he was aware, I learned
his secret likings of the Alsatian home; and the next time we sent to
town an order was given that made his material life a little more
agreeable than before. At least I so imagined, though he said
nothing.

At dinner I said, "Many people think you imagine a good many
things. They say it's all imagination about your growing, being
guided, etc." He placed his finger alongside his nose and tweaked
it, saying:

"Does imagination put a bone in a man's nose? Does imagination
change the shape of a man's head? I felt my forehead often on that
long walk and found a bump first on the left side, then the right, just
like a calf before the horns appear. Now see!" and he gave his head
a toss, throwing back the long curls and showing a well developed,

high forehead. Glancing at his feet, he continued: "Look at those feet!" You saw me cut off the tips of my shoes, for my feet are growing. These shoes will soon be too small, but you saw the other day how well prepared I am for that contingency. I have grown in height, too, several inches, and am growing now. Give me a tape measure and I will show you."

We arose and he stood in the parlor doorway and measured himself. "Six feet and still growing!" were the happy words that rang out clear and loud, accompanied by a smile of satisfaction. "Father told me I would keep on growing all the time I am away from the world."

Recalling what I had read of him, when settled for the evening, "Are you a reincarnationist?" I asked.

"No one who studies the Bible can believe otherwise. Rebirth is taught clearly in many places, and in John's Gospel he records, "Art thou Elias?' 'Art thou that prophet?' which surely proves reincarnation, and also its acceptance in that day as a spiritual truth. It is the most glorious hope of humanity today. It is the only solution of conditions, apparent inequalities, and it is the one eternal, invariable law. No chance, no accidents, no variableness. Father told me in the beginning of my walk that this is the one great truth, the vital supplement to come to the Christian world at this time, and He explained by telling me the parable of rebirth. The grain is now ripe. It has to be garnered. It must be threshed and cleaned. It has to be sized to find which has come to maturity. Earth lives are the ten sieves, which are like ten grades of lives lived since the creation of the earth. I mean TEN GOOD lives. We are reaping now what we have sown in former incarnations. Jesus taught this heavenly law, 'As ye sow ye shall reap.' For nineteen hundred years the world has known and read and preached it. But one thing, oh, world, thou lackest. Go live the Law! For that Invincible, Invisible, Unchangeable Hand is always behind the curtain and always at work. No one can enter the Kingdom who has not had ten good lives."

"That is the lowest degree," I asked, "ten lives?"

"No. I said ten good lives, for some have come and been so lukewarm that incarnation doesn't count. They are born, vegetate, marry and die; and what have they done? A life must be active, helpful, good, to count when the sifting time comes for the Kingdom. There must be growth, and there can be none in selfishness."

"Yours is a unique theosophy as life's philosophy. But tell me the maximum and minimum number of lives."

"Father says no one ego has been here less than three times nor more than three hundred. The later, the innumerable deaths of infants, mostly. How glorious to think they are all here! and the Bible characters. For I've met St. John; but John the Baptist will be killed in London in the future. Paul is here today, but not in the leading class, as the world goes. Aaron, too, is here."

"Well, he didn't do much but talk when here before. How is he now?"

"Still talking," said he, without a smile. "But let me tell you a story to illustrate the meaning. In Alsace there was born a most fearless, daring child whose parents lived near a lake. As soon as that child could toddle it was perfectly reckless, and all were looking for its untimely death. And, sure enough, one day it fell off a board and drowned. In time a babe was born to the unhappy family; the shyest, most shrinking, timid soul. Now do you see? It was the same ego that had learned its lesson. It knew more than to dare anything and everything. Death had taught it what life could not."

"To my mind, the law of heredity or pre-natal influence could account for that; it seems an easier or more natural explanation than reincarnation of the ego," I replied.

"To my mind, the law of heredity or pre-natal influence could account for that; it seems an easier or more natural explanation than reincarnation of the ego," I replied.

"You are mistaken," he reiterated; "there is no law of heredity governing the soul-development. Heredity applies merely to the physical, not the psychical."

While reading Professor Herron's article, "Opportunity of the Church," the fascination of the truth of rebirth and its practical application to today so impressed me that I asked, "Who is Professor Herron?"

"One of the reincarnated Prophets. He sees. He knows. The saints are all here, ready for the harvest time. Just think! For ages, all unconsciously, the faithful have been gathering; gathering together, slowly, surely, for the Great Day, the coming Kingdom about to be, Here and Now! Yet what business has the chaff with the wheat? As I told the deputy sheriff's wife in Hot Springs when I was cleaning out the sheriff's house — in fact, house cleaning — 'Yes, yes, I am house cleaning now with water. But wait. Later on it will be house cleaning with fire.'"

We will take his counsel and wait the fulfillment of his prophecy; for oft he repeated, "they that have ears to hear will hear! And for the others — well, it doesn't matter. Father will teach them a lesson they need, and they will know more next time."

"By the way, since Mr. Swingle is absent on the trail of that horse thief, and said he'll go to the Gulf but what he'll catch him, I'll have to go to the postoffice, for it has been nearly two weeks since any one brought the mail."

"You can drive Butte," said the Healer. "Exercise will do him good — the fat rascal. If he can jump a five-barred fence, just to visit with other horses, he can work a little, too."

So harness was put on him and I agreed to be back in four or five hours, meantime imploring him not to venture out, as cowboys were liable any moment to come over a hill or ride round a corner. It was a comfort and pleasure to drive that sensible horse. When his harness didn't fall right he stopped, looked back at me and told me, as best an animal could, to change it. At the cross road postoffice he was critically examined, being a large, fat and unbranded animal. This caused comment and confirmed suspicion that the Healer was hidden in the hills somewhere, as Butte looked strikingly like the pictures of him in the newspapers. I was back on time, and no one discovered the inmate of the home; no travelers had passed en route to Arizona. The children's letters were read with great interest.

After supper again reincarnation, with irresistible charm, came under discussion, he affirming that it "is the golden key to all mysteries." I told him the long and strange tale of trying to live the "Golden Rule" — really to get down to its very depths, and do exactly as you would be done by — unflinchingly to face the consequences, and never to look back.

"I know. Father has told me all. But you had to have every blow, every lesson, to teach you. Father has laid His hand heavily upon you, for He is disciplining you for the future. But at the same time Father always teaches a double lesson. Now, give any soul that always chose evil, power, unlimited power, say, as a ruler or leader, and what would he do? You do not see human nature as it is today. So Father taught you in a way you won't forget. What do you expect of those who have been here only five poor lives?"

The spirit of interesting and lively conversation was replaced by the inclination to read or to have me read aloud to him, from such books or periodicals only as he would permit. Often, when I thoughtlessly ventured to begin by, "Here is something fine, listen," he would say decidedly:

"No, don't read that; Father don't want to." And by observation my lesson and position had been well learned, and no words passed between us as to why not.

The back numbers of the "Arena" he especially enjoyed. One day he said so little, only answering questions in monosyllables, and yet the gravity of his thoughts was so apparent in his gestures, face and ominous silence, that finally I ventured to ask him:

"What is it you have in mind?"

"I am reading an article by Emil Richter in 'Arena,' June, 1895, 'Monopolism and Militarism,' and just listen to this:

"'The question now is the immediate restoration of order, even if the entire army of the United States must march to our relief. Brooklyn is humiliated. Its authorities are defied. It has been said again and again that the people sympathize with the strikers. That may be, but this is not the time to be weak-kneed. It is a time for firmness and determination. I want to back up the authorities. There is no time to waste upon side issues. There is but one issue. Every street in this city must be made so safe that no one policeman shall be needed in any car that runs. I wish the riot act had been read last Monday; but we are where we are, and I believe that our city authorities have acted according to their best judgement. The time has come, however, when our representatives in the city hall should know that the people are prepared for vigorous action. *If clubs will not do, then bayonets; if bayonets will not do, then lead; if lead will not do, then Gatling guns.* If we must have martial law and a state of siege, then let us have them; and if the worst comes to the worst, we will turn our churches into hospitals.'"

He sprang to his feet as the closing words of this extract were read in an increasing intensity of voice and, with eyes blazing and hand clenched, he cried out:

"He is nothing but a 'whited sepulchre' and a damnable hound!"

"Let me see the book. Who said that? Was it a preacher? A soldier of Christ?" I asked.

"A hellish 'soldier of Christ' who advocated such tyranny and slaughter!" he exclaimed and, as he paced the floor, his comments were furious in condemnation of this Brooklyn divine (?) whom Richter had quoted in his brave article defending the strikers.

Such ideas would stimulate him to the fiercest denunciation of the "greed, grind and grasp" of our era, and the pitiful condition of this stage of development by evolution. But, as the larger plan of the Creator took possession of his mind he would finally say, softly:

"I wish that day would come," referring to the universal peace of the incoming Kingdom.

"Let me read aloud Christ's Sermon," I said.

"Turn rather to the twenty-third chapter of Matthew; it's more to the point," he answered, "for there we get the list of 'Woe unto you' from the Lord Himself when He was here 1,900 years ago." Then adding again: "Did you ever hear of them stoning false prophets? Lincoln could not be bought, driven or coaxed, and what did they do to him? Was he not a true prophet?

"Do you not understand how the millionaires are made? Do you not see? What did Lincoln do with his minister of finance during the war? Don't you remember? He took down the Constitution, read it, and finally said, 'Well, if no one will loan us money we will make our own.' He then had greenbacks issued, and the war proceeded without the bankers' gold. Then the bankers went to the secretary of the treasury, or influenced the government in some way, to put in the exception clause, and after that the merchant went to the banker to get the gold for the payment of import or export duties. The banker had his interest-bearing bonds and he, in turn, went to the government for his gold; and so that gold did triple service; and that very same gold made a wheel, and God knows how many times it was sold over and over again. You see, the merchants had to pay as high as $2.85 in greenbacks for $1 in gold. And back again it goes to the bankers, as interest on the government's bonds which they hold, and which they bought with greenbacks at less than half their face value. This was the scheme the bankers had played for their own enrichment. And it goes on, intensifying in its disasters from day to day. All this time the people are paying heavy taxes, the producers are losing constantly. The moneyed few are the blood-sucking parasites on the common people.

"Look at the hypocritical mouth-worshippers of today. Has not the Church had its chance? Once the Church had all power, but what did it do? Was it true to its trust? No. It misused the trust for greed, avarice, selfishness and personal ends. It has not cared for Father's children, but for greed, covetousness, self. One and all, from the beginning, have misused power. A workingman could not enter a Fifth Avenue church unless he wore a white shirt. He could not enter their clique. He would not be admitted. But these fine ones will scheme to wreck families. And, to say it plainly, they do square robbery, and then turn and give $10,000 to some church. Father doesn't want any such damnable money. He will spew it out of his mouth. It is a terrible mistake for them to think such methods will save them from what is waiting for them; and they will have to change mighty sudden in order to save themselves. They have been reading for 1,900 years in Scripture, 'Your gold and silver is cankered, and the rust of them shall be a witness against you and shall eat your flesh as it were fire. Ye have heaped up treasure for the last days!' But do they believe it?

"Tariff is a smoke only — a sham battle to make smoke so that the people can't see the real issue. Everybody knows that; for when Cleveland went in what became of the tariff? Congress went to work on silver destruction. England had a hand in that. Did not the English bankers tell us to abolish chattel slavery? They knew that when you own the money of a nation you own all that labor produces. Workers are then industrial slavers, which is a surer, a more permanent slavery. Chattel slaves they had to feed, clothe, house and care for when sick. How is the industrial slave? They put him out of doors. They don't care if he has or has not.

"They made the nation drunk with that cup of fornication — with that dollar, that almighty dollar, that damnable dollar!

"Which are the more degraded — chattel or industrial slaves? I want no misunderstanding. There are classes and classes of wage workers. Ah, yes! There are the self-sold slaves; they are a different class from the industrial slaves. The latter are now helpless, I know. Have I not been one? Did I not sit at the bench twenty-three years? Never forget I was a workingman. It's the devilish system! It's the cursed institution, and those who uphold it will reap their reward. If they sow the wind they will reap the whirlwind. That is the law from on high. Have they clothed the naked, fed the hungry? Have they housed the homeless? Have they protected the widow and orphan?

"There has been no peace since Adam. Is not 6,000 years enough? How long must they suffer? But the day cometh when the promises for thousands of years shall be fulfilled. He will show the world unmistakably that He is the Lord their God and they are His people. Then we shall have peace once and forever.

"There are only a handful of ripe souls, and the few must not compromise. A compromise always shows little faith, a weakness of faith in the Father. No matter how few the chosen ones, they should never make a compact. No alliances! For, as I can take this pitcher and dash it to pieces there, so can Father dash the nations — crush them, when they do not His will. Whenever a compact is made the weaker always get deceived. Perfidy is the policy of the stronger; the faithful, being good themselves, believe in the honesty of the stronger. Just look at history! Well, it has been 6,000 years of deception. The strong today say, 'We have all the ships, men and money.' But all the ships, arms and money will not save them, because the nations have sowed iniquities, they will reap their reward. What you sow you reap. Has He not promised through all the ages to establish His Kingdom? Has He not said in His Word. 'There is One coming?'' He did send Him, and what did they do? Now, this time, they will have no chance.

"When His time comes He will bring me back. There is only a handful of faithfuls. But those who will not want to hear the Voice will be the three classes — thieves, liars and hypocrites. These three classes have all in their hands today. They have all; and, by deceit, lying and theft, keep all.

"I had to follow the Father to learn and then to teach, that there is One who cares for nothing only cold Justice. Jesus taught, talked and preached. His life was all words of love, kindness ethical laws. Now it's deeds, not words, the Father demands. To the everlasting shame of humanity they crucified Jesus. But Father lets do.

"Jesus was the Lamb of God — but this time He has sent the Lion of the tribe of Judah. Of myself, I can do nothing. I am utterly powerless — helpless. Alone I can do nothing. With Him I can do all things — whatever the Father commands — all He wants done.

"Jesus came to establish the Kingdom, but by His death the suffering has been continued 1,900 years longer. But they would not. They must come into the Kingdom of their own free will. Father will not force them.

"Study those three classes — the thieves, liars, hypocrites! These three brought on the conditions. Thieves — colossal thieves — made the tramp, prostitute and drunkard. The hyprocrite poses as a saint, then turns around and robs the whole community. If an honest man arises and tries to better things, they shout the cry, 'Oh, these things always have been, and they always will be; you can't change things;' at the same time slyly drawing in that dollar and getting the people deeper in, day by day. Oh! I wish the day come! It will! He has promised it for ages. The stubble and the chaff have no business with the grain. The barn floor will be cleansed with fire. When they come back the next time they will know more. Spiritual things are limitless. To cleanse is a law of Spirit.

"Look at the earth. How beautiful! He has given all they need to His children — flowers, fruits, birds, metals, soil, sunshine, trees — all life, and the rain in its season. But they are all here — saints and devils! Yes, all, for such a time as this — saints and devils. And those in power in these man-made institutions are devils. They are possessed of the Spirit of Evil to crush, rob, and deceive the believing. No man who wants to do right has a chance, for he is soon trampled under. If a man is too honest they get him out of the way somehow or other, either by corruption, scaring him, or, by some method, he is quietly put out of their path if he refuses to be a tool. For that dollar, of course, the self-sold slave will do dirty work — become a willing tool. How many have lived up to their highest? Had they, what necessity for me to walk — to wander on that weary pilgrimage — that indescribable agony? That was my university and I learned my lesson well — for I care only for cold Justice.

"The day of Jesus' teaching has been fulfilled. Something else has been divinely ordered. Jesus talked, persuaded — He taught heavenly love. Do they live the Lord's prayer, or only say it with their mouths one day in seven?"

The Healer had talked along these lines for hours, and it seemed foreboding. Perhaps it was fitting to call his mind to the few forces in this age that make for righteousness. The schools, colleges, universities, some churches, women's and workingmen's organizations, the pure homes, and the reform press were all recounted to him as living up to their highest, at least. But with a sudden halt and uplifted arm, he said, more vehemently, if possible, than before:

"Have there not been some such institutions always? There was culture in Jesus' day. What did they do with Jesus? Sent Him on a journey — and a forcible one, too! Ellis Meredith says people act as if God had gone on a journey. Father has always been ready and willing and ever present, but they would not. Well, next times they will know better."

"Why did you not publish this to the world last year in Denver?" I asked.

"It would not do that they knew I had another mission than healing. I had to be still. The hypocrites, have they not done a still work for centuries? Have those in power not robbed the nations one after another? But when Father brings His servant He will bring him with power to crush out the wicked and restore the stolen goods to whom they belong, and put the teachings of Jesus into practice. And there shall be no houseless, hungry, shoeless, unclothed, when the Kingdom has come."

"Then we are to believe Jesus was a social reformer as well as teacher?" I queried.

"Yes. Professor Herron is a prophet. He sees. Some of his writings are of the right thought, at least those I have seen since reading The Arena here, on the Religion of Jesus; for His religion was radical, reformatory, reaching all humanity. How can it be other than Socialism, when He gave the Golden Rule? Is that Golden Rule something about the stars and solar systems? Or is it a social rule for humanity to live up to?"

"You have told us about a meeting in Denver of what I choose this time to call the 'Wise Men of the West' — and being questioned there, etc., the time Mr. Reed sat on your left hand, and another on your right. Did they not ask about your future?" I enquired.

"Ah, yes. But I told them the head of the serpent lies in London and that it has its coils around the world, and that nothing but the Creator Himself can crush it. London is the modern Babylon, the

Babylon mentioned in Revelations. The Beast is the Money Power, no matter where found. It is always one and the same. Mammon worship is in the Church as well as in State and Society at large. Yet it is a unit. The Gold Power is one combine. You will live to see. Mark my words well. The Serpent is tightly coiled, and man can't break his coils. Mankind has been asleep too long. Now it is too late. The last days are upon the earth. They will be forced to look to Father for relief — for escape. But they are all here — all here."

I replied, "It seems you mean something like what we were once taught about the great battle of Armageddon described in the sixteenth chapter of Revelations — Evil on one side, Good on the other. Is that what you mean by 'all here, all here?'"

"I mean the Lord's Prayer is to be answered right here upon this earth. I mean the day has nearly gone by when we will ask, 'Thy Kingdom come, Thy will be done', for it will be here, and we won't have to pray for that for another 1,900 years. Isn't that a long enough time to be asking for one thing, the Kingdom of Heaven? Jesus would not teach a lie, would He? Father keeps His promises."

"Yes, doubtless," I replied, "but it doesn't seem He answers prayer these days as in ancient times. It seems worlds were sent whirling through space and then, to most of us, 'God did take a journey.'"

"Father does not often act directly in human affairs," he replied. "Biblical history shows how often; but when He does, they have cause to remember it a long time. For myself , I never would have said one word. Ah, no! It would not take me ten minutes to decide what to do. They have been, and will be, given a long time to think and decide whether His Hand is in the affairs of men; but look how they treat those who want to do righteously. Look at Debs! — that strike against Corporate Power; his illegal imprisonment! Was Debs right or wrong? Do such corporation leaders follow Jesus' teachings?

"You say this is election year, and ask, 'What of this nation?' Political methods will not now help humanity. It has gone too far. The people didn't see quickly enough. It is too late. I say this: The Gold Powers will win one way or another. Don't you see? They will never voluntarily let go. Did not a New York man say, 'The people be damned!' and another New Yorker say, 'We can hire one-half to kill the other half?' Are the common people united like the Mammonites? Look at the Gold Worshippers. Suppose ballots enough are counted this fall to give the people liberty, do you not think England will send help to New York? They are one in the spirit of greed the world over. They won't let go; so there is no help for humanity save the Spiritual Forces that are greater than all the materialistic methods or powers.

"This nation of the West is going down faster than any nation of all history. Look at its unparalleled opportunities! It is almost an un-discovered land — a youth, as nations grow — yet see a few men own its wealth today! A few men actually control the lands, foods, necessities of all other men. Think of that high-handed robbery! Do you think that is the Divine plan? This nation ought to have no poor, no hungry, no downtrodden. But the spirit of evil is here and has accomplished more since your war than ever before. The enslave-ment has been more rapid. Conditions are horrible; common people are robbed of what Father wanted them to have. Consider the Spiritual aid given to Washington and others in his infancy, for it seemed to give promise then. But look now! Where is righteousness?"

So spake the man of mighty faith — the only one that lives the life and has the faith of Jesus.

As the weeks glided into months he continually repeated his expressions of gratitude. "Father is good to me. I did not expect it when I came. I did not think He would let me stay so long, but it has a double purpose." Then, leisurely glancing at the center table, he commented on some books there. "Science and Health," "Blossom of the Century," "Key to Theosophy," and "Ideal Suggestion," each in its turn, and he closed by saying:

"People read too much. You would have been more highly developed, spiritually, had you read less and meditated and thought more. Let go of books, merely the thoughts of other people. In 1892 I read Mental Science, but it only woke me up. Then I had to throw it overboard and follow the Father. How full of theories some people are! But have the beauties of the thirty-fifth chapter of Isaiah been fulfilled? Read it and see. The prophecies have not been fulfilled and will not be till the Kingdom has been established on earth. I have told you of my vision of the wars that are coming. I've been shown many ships going down, down, carrying with them every one on board."

"Humanity has certainly outgrown war," I suggested. "All disagreements can be peacefully settled without bloodshed, surely, at this late day."

"No. You express a hope, but look at cold facts. Look at Europe. How about Armenia and Turkey? There comes in that financial question again. England, so called a Christian nation, allows Armenia to be butchered. Why? Don't you see where the Damnable Dollar plays the chief part again? Turkey owes England money and,

therefore, in order to collect her interest, she can easily see innocent lives lost rather than interfere, for then Turkey might not pay
up. See? If Armenia had any money the world would see England's
power come down and stop this horrible business in twenty-four
hours."

"Yes," I replied, "that is the way you look behind effects and constantly teach anew the Gospel lesson that 'The Love of money is the
root of all evil;' only you make it so decidedly short by saying 'that
damnable dollar.' Your estimate, in its universal application and its
widespread ramifications, can scarcely be believed till you point
out the monster iniquity at every turn. You see its hideous head all
down the ages and in every national history."

"Yes, I have studied history ever since I could read, and before
that. As I sat on my father's loom he told me stories of the French
Revolution, and how our ancestors suffered, and the woes of war.
Moreover, my father explained causes to me, taught me the reasons
of things, and led me to see the wicked ways of the leaders; how little they care for the masses; how, for the foible of a king, because he
is a ruler, the common people are massacred by thousands; how
few protest or think seriously of the right or wrong of it. Humanity
has to do its own thinking. They are old enough to begin now, for
it's only by their own thinking that they grow spiritually."

These talks were given in sincerity amounting at times almost to
vehemence. With religious fire he was fairly frenzied over conditions. In fact, one could hear him think. His whole mental make-up
was intensely in earnest. He paced the floor habitually and volleys
of words came forth.

"I will soon be away with Father alone. He would rather have me
with wild beasts than human beasts. Then the time will come when
they can spend the millions they have taken from the poor and unfortunate, in trying to hunt me. But they can never find me."

"When you are called away," I asked, "where do you expect to
go? I mean, in which direction?"

"I shall go where Father takes me, but I must be alone. He often
told me I must go to the Soudan, and that the 144,000 must be taken
out of Egypt. And at first I thought I had to cross the seas. Now I
know different. Egypt is on this continent and the 144,000 are reincarnated in the western hemisphere. But I must follow the Father
and He will do the rest."

He began to walk and sing the "Marseillaise," and then stopped
in front of the fireplace, saying:

"I am the happiest man in creation. As they said in Denver, I have
the greatest responsibility of any one, though only forty years old.

But I know these terrible years of humanity are coming to a rapid and unexpected close. Father told me in the beginning of my walk that I have a greater work to do than Moses, and I wish the day would come."

He sang a long time, and the hymn must have revived early memories, for he began to tell me stories of his life in Paris, saying, with quaint humor and queer expressions:

"I wanted to enlist in the French army during the Franco-Prussian war, and the government official asked me questions and unwarrantedly said bluntly, 'You are a Prussian!' Aye! Was I wild? Was I not? He then asked more questions, as who 'opted' for me, or who chose for me? My brother, who lived in Alsace, was my guardian, as father and mother were dead, and he could not choose for me, for fear of persecution from the Prussians. I was too young, they said, to have option; but he repeated, 'You are a Prussian.' I rose in my indignation and said, 'Before I'll go in the German army I'll go to America! I thought of all I had lost for my principle. The Jew had all my inheritance, but I never obey that dollar when a principle is at stake. To think of all I had sacrificed, and that my sisters had told me never to call myself brother again if I went with the French in that war! Then to have a govenment official tell me that! I then said, 'I'm going to London to complete my study of English, and thence go to America.' And I did, as fast as I could execute the plan, and work at the same time fourteen hours a day. Speaking of my life in Paris recalls my mother's deathbed at our cottage home in Ebersheim, at noon on a Sunday — 16th of April, 1871. She probably knew for days the outcome, but did not speak of it till. Saturday night. While I was alone with her in her room, between daylight and dark, she called me to her bedside, saying, 'Francis, come here. I have something to say to you.' I can see the room now, the flickering firelight, the shadows, and her face on the pillow. She then said, 'This is my last night upon earth. You are very young. I want you to promise me never to go to a city, never. I can not die with that thought, that you will leave home and go to a great city; for the vanities of the world, the vices and temptation may overcome you. And, above all, never change your religion. Live true to the one faith always. Stay here in the homestead all your remaining years, and you and your sisters will then be safe. Before I die you must know how I feel. I shall not be able ever to speak to you again of my wishes.'"

He sighed as he went into the details of this lonely death scene, and said how often he thought he saw his mother in his miserable life in Paris; for circumstances drove him to the very city life she so dreaded. But he consoled himself, saying to his mother, 'Had you not died I should indeed never have left Alsace. I would always have remained with you, as long as you lived, but your death changed all things, and I was forced to leave the village, adrifted to Paris, then London, finally America."

He sung other songs in French, then relapsed into silence and deep and profound thought, as he paced rapidly back and forth. I went out on the front porch to look at the majestic mountains in the quiet moonlight and thanked the poet for saying.

"For the majesty of mountains,
I thank Thee, O, my God!"

After he had been alone a long time I went back and said:

"Come out and look at the quiet beauty of the scene tonight. It's sublime. The shadows of the tall pines on the mountain sides, the soft light of the moon and the stars! It is rarely magnificent."

"No. I don't care to see it. On my walk I used to want to talk to Father about the stars and astronomy, but He told me to keep my mind on the earth a while longer; that the earth had to be straightened out first; that after the work was done I would have plenty of time to study the stars and look at the beauties of Nature. I've had enough scenery to satisfy me on that long tramp across the continent."

Some days later we were reading the newspapers, though several weeks old, and they contained the account of the Chicago Woman's Christian Temperance Union refusing to allow Robert G. Ingersoll the privilege of free speech in a certain hall. The fact was thought-provoking, and out came the valued scrap book that I might read aloud Ingersoll's address to a jury on the temperance question — one of the most eloquent perorations in our language; also other things he had said on the liberty of woman and the rights of children. Here I tried again to reconcile women's words with their deeds. Ingersoll had ever championed woman's liberty and the cause of temperance, yet these people seemed to be afraid one man could demolish a so-called divine institution by more talk. That evening Mr. Swingle brought up an old paper with the latest lecture in it by the noted heretic, and I saw a good opportunity to test the Healer's breadth of mind and to prove the beauty of his tolerant spirit. At breakfast the next day I drew forth the paper, saying, "Here is Ingersoll's latest. Would you like to hear it?"

"Certainly. Read it. Father says he is a man of great faith; only the professing Christians have given him too much material to use against religion by their hyprocrisy and mouth worship. Had they lived the principles Jesus taught, Mr. Ingersoll would have found fewer facts and less insincerity to hold up to scorn, and he would not have had the chance to say so much. And the pity is, too much of what he says is true. Father says he has faith in the Unseen Forces and is ready for the impending change. But let me hear his lecture."

I read it, interspersed with keen comments of the lone auditor as each paragraph was finished. He knew what Ingersoll had called him, but that did not, in the least, prejudice or affect his just judgement of one man.

In this connection an allied event appropriately comes in and illustrates his remarkable memory. One Sunday, sitting under a towering tree, he commenced to tell of his London life, and particulary the Sunday afternoons in Hyde Park, where he frequently listened to John Burns' lectures to the laboring men, and he repeated with astonishing accuracy and detail, notwithstanding the many intervening years, the one in which Burns described how he had found Thomas Paine's "Rights of Man" by accident on the shores of Africa while the ship was in port. And, from this retrospect, presently sank into his usual serious mood, saying:

"Preaching is a life, not a business. When the call comes the world must be sacrificed. Jesus was a celibate. And look at the Apostles, though all of them are on the earth today again. But for spiritual work there must be sacrifice of self and of the world. Teaching and preaching must be for the uplift of humanity. It is not a business nor on the material plan, but to help humanity, and has always meant self-sacrifice and always will till the Kingdom comes. Yes, the Quakers are right in that they don't pay their preachers or leaders. Father gives them the light freely, and freely they must give, if honest. That is the real thing. No money — no money mixed with spiritual enlightenment."

III.

A March Monday found the Healer still with us, pleasant as possible. The breakfast over, and the recurrence of the mystic numbers in his name and in the events of his life having been frequently referred to, it was entertaining, to to say the least, to make out or systematize them. So I began:

"Do you know how often the mystic numbers 3, 7, 10 occur in your history?"

"No. I never think about such things. How do you mean?"

I replied, "Well, for instance, Francis has 7 letters, Schlatter, 9. You were born the 9th hour on the 29th day of April, 1856. You were fourteen years old when your father died. You see two 7's, don't you. The events then seem to run in even numbers till your spiritual birth. But after you landed in America it changes, as you will see. You reached Denver on the 19th of the 9th month. When 37 years old you had your vision in the 3rd month. You started to walk on the 19th of the 7th month of 1893. I don't recall enough of your walk — I mean dates, for you give none — to figure out mystic numbers. But you began your 40-days' fast in the 7th month. You were in Denver nearly 3 months. Left on a 13th; traveled 7 weeks and 6 days, and stopped on the 7th at the 7th white person's house en route south. In being permitted to enter certain houses as a temporary guest, after your 730 days' walk, you were in 3 religious divisions: Protestant, Catholic, and a lost Truth Seeker, and we are sure you will be permitted to remain 3 months with us in this year of our Lord, '96. These are, you see, a few illustrations to show you my meaning."

"When you have leisure won't you read some account of those Indian Adepts? It is very interesting to me, and their mode of life. I've always wanted to go to India, and Father says I shall, when His work is complete on this side." That afternoon was spent as he asked, and in the evening the conversation turned on personal matters. He had often looked at a photograph of one very dear to me; had stood listening to the Voice, inaudible to others, and he spoke very seriously:

"Father says he was very spiritual." The memory of his great nature and courageous life passed before me; and yet, with the years of intimate friendship, it never would have occured to me to apply "spiritual" to such a one. Therefore I said:

"Brave, loyal, loving, long suffering, yes; but I can't see where 'spiritual' is descriptive of such a man and, moreover, he rarely ever entered a church."

He smiled as he replied, "Father says he always did the best he knew how, and is here now."

"Well, if reincarnate, he is only thirteen years of ago, as you arrived on the thirteenth anniversary of his funeral. If I am ever to know him beyond the grave I feel confused as to the way."

"In Father's time all things will be revealed. My mother is now reincarnate in Mexico, and some day I shall see her. She died twenty-five years ago, but I know she is in Mexico."

This and other evenings were spent in talks of the family, lastly adding:

"It is not often I care to hear personal or business troubles, for Father knows all hearts. But when I hear of treachery and robbery it makes me more determined than ever," and he began to pace the spacious room, reverting to the political conditions and the utter futility of political methods now. It brought up the possible purification of politics by the on-coming universal suffrage, and the reserve moral force now disfranchised. He stopped short in front of me, asking doubtfully:

"Women vote in several states, and what have they accomplished? Have they changed things? Of course they have a right to vote, but what good has it done up to date? I tell you, political methods won't do! Only the limitless spiritual forces can now help humanity. They will see. If you want to know of the times in which we live go back to your Bible. Read it with the key you have, and you can understand the reason that it is too late to remedy things by man-made laws."

Next to political liberty, or mayhap it rightfully takes precedence, is physical liberty allowed by natural dress. "What do you think of woman's mode of dress?" I ventured. I saw I had struck a key note by that question, and he talked an hour in reply, commencing:

"How can women be free when they can not overcome fashion? That is the first thing they ought to do, for in following the fashion they lose health, strength and independence. Some fool for money sets the mode; they all follow, so that same fellow can make the money out of their nonsense. Women's present dress is all nonsense. Of course birds on hats are folly. Some man in Paris usually does their thinking for them, but why do they not go the modiste and say, 'I want comfort, and I propose to have it. Do this way or another, for I will have it no other.' I do my own thinking, and when women sacrifice artificial things and live nearer Nature, Father will heal them rapidly. How can they pray in a tight-laced corset? And heels! If Father wanted us to have heels He would have put bumps on our feet. These fashionables are somewhat like me on that walk — they haven't enough vitality to live and too much to die. But, like everything else, dress is ruined in every way, shape and manner. Next to Nature is best. It's the only right way."

This day's talks had proved how eminently sane the former shoemaker was on these lines and, consequently rejoicing, I was impelled to reply.

"In the Kingdom, if I am permitted to live out of door as I do here, I understand that we can have liberty to abolish superfluous dry goods, in fact, to do as we please."

The very mention of the Kingdom always elated him, and he smiled as he commenced to devote another hour to the architecture of the houses in the New Time. He said, "They are to be of equable temperature, tile floors, both heated and ventilated by means of pipes from below, never of more than one story, but forty feet or more high, in order to get pure air. And the rare, beautiful materials in these ideal homes, where no one shall want, and justice reign supreme! For the idealistic era is approaching. And the roads!"

Then he told how the Europeans are greatly in advance of us, saying that the roads in the Kingdom will surpass any the earth has ever seen. Then came under discussion nutritious kinds of food and physical culture. Each kindred subject he picked up, treated and dismissed in its turn, with force, precision and perspicuity.

"This is Sunday," I said. "Won't you go with us driving up the Left Hand canyon? But ask Father first if you will be safe."

"Father says no one will come today." Hence one of the few extensive airings and long drives permitted by his Guide was taken, without resulting in the discovery of his presence by curiosity seekers or bringing other disastrous consequences to his peaceful life.

The days were drawing on apace when we were to prepare for his departure. But with the thought came the dread of his renewed sufferings and awful agony, alone in the mountains. He talked less, ate less, but slept more. He told us not to disturb him for the meals, that he preferred to sleep, and periods of fourteen or sixteen hours' continuous rest were not infrequent during the last three weeks.

One day the "Arena Art Folio" that was lying on the table attracted my attention and, inviting him to stop walking and sit down by the open fire, as I handed him the pictures I asked an opinion of the real characters. If Jesus made two great classes of humanity, denominated believers and unbelievers, Schlatter did the same under newer names — prejudiced and unprejudiced — though "faithful" was the more common word for unprejudiced. It was startling, and rather upset my preconceived notions of certain celebrities to have him say, "prejudiced, full of it," about a noted woman leader, though he did not recognize the face; then, again, "ambitious, has not had ten good lives." In fact, from the evening's experience, I know he asks the Father only one question when a person or picture is in front of him, "How many good lives has he had?" If they have not chosen at least nine good lives before, this being the tenth chance to choose the good, he is sublimely indifferent to them, deeming it useless to try, talk to or treat them. One woman he called spiritual, although this world calls her an infidel. Silently I lingered long with "Folio" in my lap, pondering over his strange way and sayings. How singularly he sees subjects and people all from one point: Reincarnation! No other thought seems to occupy his mind when estimating life and the present effects from that unseen cause. "Of course," he always affirmed, "I of myself could never tell a faithful from a prejudiced except I ask Father and He tells me; then I always know the hidden character. After the faithful come the chosen ones. Ah! how few, all in the hollow of His hand. But the chosen will help to straighten out this world and its false standards and wicked conditions. But they must be the real thing, the tried, the true. They are highly unfolded, spiritually. They don't worship Mammon. They love God; and you know Jesus said you can't do both. You have to abandon one or the other. Prejudice forbids clear sight. If you say, 'Thou fool,' that is the beginning of prejudice, and that is the worst thing. There can be nothing worse than prejudice. Don't say 'fool', simply because another can not understand. Moreover, Jesus wanted His followers to come to perfection, and a man can never come to perfection under prejudice. He must drop that. And to those of faith? Faith must be unflinching. I don't mean zeal, for it is momentary. Faith is steady and forever constant."

"Tell me," I interrupted, "about that threatened kinship cannibalism in Leviticus, and where is the justice of God in His being partial to the Jews?"

"God wasn't partial to the Jews. It was the Jews who were partial to God. He tried all nations before the Jews. Abraham did the will of the Father. You know that history. With a high hand He put them out of Egypt. He could have taken them out in forty days instead of forty years, but they rebelled. They disdained the promised land. They were afraid. They were of little faith. For disobedience they were in that desert, and those of mature years were not allowed to live. Father's law is one of penalty for violation. That idea is all through Scripture, either sudden or slow. No one knows His ways. When enough is suffered He removes the penalty and gives another chance. Had He not forgiveness and long forbearance He would have smashed up this earth long ago, for the children have continued to break His laws. The good things they disdain, and usually make bad use of His good gifts. 'He doesn't give us anything,' says the world, 'and if I don't get that dollar, I can't have anything.' But the door is always open. Whosoever will may come, if they are ready. He is willing to forgive, but they don't want to listen. They want nothing but their own way."

"But the first part of my question?" I said.

"Why, the race was in its infancy then. When that part of the Old Testament was written the world was like a twelve-year-old boy. It was crude, and the people had to be taught by forceful methods.

Father says often that I am only an eighteen-year-old child, but I am growing, and I will grow through all eternity."

While the Old Testament was under consideration I was still in a critical, almost cynical, mood, and asked him if polygamy was a Divine institution. He turned with strangely lit eyes and, by way of answer, gave me another question, saying:

"Do you suppose Father approves what they call monogamy today, with its prevalent hypocrisy? Is the present marriage system Divine in its meaning and methods? Don't understand me to attack marriage, or wholly disapprove it; but look at the hypocrisy of the system generally. Up to now it has served its purpose, but Father will teach something far better in the Kingdom. It will be Justice, first."

"Yes, I know one of Jesus' historians conditioned only two things to be overcome — death and matrimony. Then we are ready for the Kingdom, but I thought we had to die in the body to overcome such formidable obstacles." When I had finished the sentence he seriously replied:

"You are up in that sycamore tree looking at a sky heaven. Jesus said, 'Come out of the tree.' You better come down from your sky heaven, for heaven is on this earth, and I am going to live one thousands years, Father says."

"The several schools of the Scientists also teach immortality in the flesh or perpetual youth; moreover, Heaven here and now," I said.

"As to Science, I know little. I had to follow the Father. No more books; no more earthly authority; simply to obey."

"When the Kingdom comes, what about schools? They are institutions of slavery to books."

"True, but Froebel's methods will be used till the pupils are twenty years of age. Teachers will take a band of young folks and go traveling. They will study Nature and her methods, and thus languages will be easily acquired."

"It will take a mint of money for that surely," I said.

"No, no. Before that day there will have been such an overturning and razing to the ground that we can then go in air ships. Inventors will increase and multiply when all barriers are swept to atoms. The gifted and the good will then have a chance. But look! How is it now? What chance is there now for an honest man? But after the chaff and wheat have been separated, talent can unfold as the lily of the field. But they are all here, all here."

Every day I heard that until I knew that the Alpha and Omega of his teachings is reincarnation, rebirth, and this closing century finds them all in, the flesh, ready for the great contest, which he predicts.

"When I think of the past, with its saints, I also remember the Herods, Neros, Caligulas, not to mention Ananias, whose spirits must have multiplied for this epoch. Are they, too, here in the flesh?" I asked.

"To be sure. Why not? They are to have a final chance and choice, and the oncoming fierce war will settle it for a thousand years. Of course, as usual, the devils of history have all material powers in their hands today. The faithful must show that all earthly powers are as nothing compared to faith in the Father. For nothing but the Creator Himself can now save the race from utter slavery and oppression. Governments today are corrupt through and through, national, state and municipal, from north to south, from ocean to ocean. Where, then, has a reformer any chance? The world is on a commercial basis; and tell me what is commerce? It is piracy on the high seas of man-made traffic. This exchange business is legalized robbery. It's too late, too late for any material remedy. Look at the English in India! Look at the tyranny! While I was in Paris I constantly read histories, and I remember them well, for history is my favorite study. Look at the history of the "Wars of India," and how England robbed the natives of their rice and then shipped it back at extortionate rates to collect unjust taxes. If you want to know how England has shamefully abused her power ever since she became a nation, go read her history. No matter where or at what time, she has always been brutal, oppressive and intolerant, and all because of that damnable dollar! But Father lets do!"

"Tell me your favorite authors."

"Louis Fiquier's Marvels of Science; and every Frenchman loves Victor Hugo; history of Rome, Egypt and Greece; wars of India and Italia; Telemaque, by a Bishop, written for Louis XV; history of the war of '70-'71; and many radical French writers. After I arrived here, in 1884, I read newspapers for a season, then Patrick Ford's Letters to Gladstone. But the one book that I shut up with myself in my shop and went without food till finished was Caesar's Column. I was greatly interested. And I believe it is prophetic, too."

That was too much and I protested quickly, saying:

"Rather let 'Looking Backward' be the prophecy. Bellamy sees the necessity for change, but his idea is not so horribly cruel as in 'Caesar's Column.' The end is the same in both hands — peace and plenty for all — but their methods are diametrically opposed."

"Have patience and faith," was the soft answer. "Father will help us out. But 'Caesar's Column' is nearer the truth than 'Looking

Backward.' But give up all books. Turn to your Bible. Go back to your Bible and learn there the truth. We are living in Revelations and are soon to enter a new dispensation," he answered.

"Well, have we not outgrown the Old Testament? Jesus claimed that He was in advance of Moses, for after quoting Moses He always began, 'But I say unto you.'"

"No, no. We will never outgrow the Law. We are still under the Law, though they don't admit it to themselves. The Bible is the spiritual history of the race, and humanity will never outgrow it."

Seeing how implicitly he relied upon the Scriptures, I asked him what was the trouble with those Denver preachers who were so bitter toward him, and he replied:

"It would seem that they ought to have been only too happy to see one living the life they had been preaching about for centuries. The churches are the very ones that ought to recognize the life, the real thing, when they see it. But they were prejudiced. As to the doctors, of course they were in the opposition, for it touched their pockets, where that dollar is. So the doctors and the preachers are the two classes that opposed the work in Denver, and it won't be long till some others will join them, but I have nothing to fear, nothing. Of myself alone I can do nothing. But with the Father I can do all things. Oh, I wish the day come! It will be quicker than some of them think; and happy are those who are not obedient to that dollar."

Some days later, his attitude was cheerful again. He sang a great deal, would go over to the barn for Butte, and was so agile and quick in his movements that I made some comments. But he must have known it, for he recalled his name in Hot Springs jail, "Cyclone," and laughed at the idea.

Moreover, he had made so many remarks to me on personal matters that I felt I could in like manner speak to him without being rude. The changing shape of his head he often talked of. Therefore, one day I called his attention to what would be, from worldly ideas, a defect. "You have no back head, Love of home, friends and country is lacking. In the motive power of affection you are deficient."

"Well, why should I have affection? I have no home, friends or country now. When Father wants me to have those qualities, my head will change in the back as it has in the front. Some day I'll have a home and country. It may be a hundred years, but when Father gives me a home and country I will love them."

The ideal of a personal God I felt borne in upon me so constantly that I asked bluntly, "Is God person or principle?"

"Both," he answered. "God is personal in His Kingdom, for

Father has a Kingdom of His own; but His Spirit permeates the universe."

I said nothing, only wondering how that could be. Conversely the power of evil naturally presented itself. Some think evil has equal power. I queried:

"What is your idea of the devil?"

"It's like a chained dog. He can't bite you if you don't go near him; or, as Revelations have it, he is and he isn't. As to have equal power with the Father — no, no, no. He's a great reasoner, that same little boy, for I reasoned with him myself every day after I came out of Hot Springs and when in California, for the little boy would say to me, 'You! you poor shoemaker; you never heal. It's all illusion. You! You can't do anything.' So you see I know that same little reasoner. But Father will always give you the will power to overcome if you ask for it, and you will get divine strength when you need it."

The practical religious duties came in always for a fair share of the time, the things that here and now demand attention. Hence, as Mr. Moore's Brochure was on the desk, and its tone being as radical as the most advanced could wish, one day I asked him if Father would allow him to hear it.

"Yes, Read."

He listened attentively to "Why I am a Vegetarian," and the ethics taught were indisputable. But he insisted that the masses were not ready to give up flesh eating, and that it would have to be a slow process, a gradual change to vegetables. He spoke of how easy it was for him to go months in jail without meat, explaining that Father took away the appetite for meat. This subject was canvassed pro and con, as had been scores of others, and finally resulted in the agreement that everybody who wanted to eat flesh ought to have the right to run a back-door private slaughter house, which custom would most effectually lessen deaths in the dumb world. He closed by saying to us that this was secondary, for social reconstruction came first; in fact, was upon us, and these minor problems would be self-adjusting in the coming Utopia. All winter he never wearied of talking of thinking of the mighty troubles which must precede the peaceful Kingdom. He permitted me also to read "Pushed by Unseen Hands," or part of it. Than the talk drifted and became desultory.

"What's a heathen?" I asked him.

"A heathen? Commonly accepted as one who doesn't speak English or other so-called civilized tongues. What are the heathens? The greedy money lover, the prejudiced. They may be even among

the shepherds, the 'fat cattle' of Scripture; they are the heathen."
And from that he again went over the situation, economically and
politically, with fire and vehemence, as he thought of the faithful.
With a masterful pose, one foot firmly planted ahead of the other,
the body leaning impressively forward, one uplifted hand half closed, the other hanging listlessly by his side, with face strangely lit
with earnest emotion, he almost wailed:

"Jesus said the meek shall inherit the earth. Do they? Who owns
the earth? Is it the meek? But God has promised it."

No one ever saw a more commanding attitude or listened to such
burning questions. It was clear that he could be eloquent and an
orator, if he chose. And, later on, he said Father had told him when
he returned he would speak in public, but they wouldn't care much
to hear what he had to say. All conversation was on the line of injustice. Helen Hunt's book, "A Century of Dishonor," came to mind
and, as usual, he had thought out the wrongs portrayed therein. He
knew much on the reservation question, how our government had
betrayed the Indian and closed by this indictment:

"The white man's scheme was to buy their lands. At the very
same time he knew he would soon manage to have back that pur-
chase money also. Then he would have both. He knew that in the
beginning of the business deal. Then where is the innocent victim?
Is that Christ-like?"

"The Indians won't kill or eat bear," I said, "at least these about
here do not. Moreover, they give as a reason that the bear is the
reincarnated brother. Even they have a dim idea of reincarnation."

"Father says it's not a dim idea. They know. But my work will not
be finished until the time when all color and creeds are liberated
from the Bondage of Hell."

His vehemence was only equal by Jesus in the twenty-third
chapter of Matthew, and to quote some little verses was a temptation. This thought was uppermost: May not a cobbler be a spiritual
giant? This man's ways and words suggested terrible interrogations
of all kinds at all times. The song of the Pagan, sojourning in
Galilee, A. D 32, tells the heart desire of many:

"If Jesus Christ is a man —
    And only a man — I say
That of all mankind I cleave to Him,
    To Him will I cleave alway.

"If Jesus Christ is a God —
    And the only god — I swear
I will follow Him through heaven and hell,

The earth, the sea, the air."

He turned to us and spoke, "Father has sent His servant again to take from the rulers and robbers the stolen goods and restore them to the faithful and meek of the earth who have been trampled upon for centuries."

It was positively painful to see his intensity, he being the soul of simplicity and sincerity. However, the conversation was adroitly turned to the World's fair sights; but that also proved pathetic. In describing the pictures I related how a Philadelphia artist had called my attention to one of Mary after the Crucifixion. Hopeless pain was there pictured in the face of agony, as the crown of thorns lay upon her lap. John and James, presumably, were on either side trying to comfort her. It had left an indelible impression on my mind, and I told him all the details. I looked up and the Healer was weeping. "Oh! that crown of thorns!" said he. One other time he shed tears because of a contemptuous remark that was made about one of the unfortunate classes of earth's humbler inhabitants. He was tender to a degree unsuspected, when discoursing on religious lines of life or experience. Abruptly he turned again to the analysis of the world, saying:

"Society is a painted shell! Civilization or society is described by two words — Oppression and Debauchery. Rank or riches can not dazzle my insight. I care not for Plutocracy's life and methods. Man has lived, does live, unrighteously, Man-made institutions must be razed to their very foundations. Thrones, princedoms, powers must be overthrown, for they stand in the path of the race to rise higher. Nothing material can stop the evolution; and nothing material can adequately express eternal or spiritual beauty and power. I see the wars coming, international, marine and, in America, between labor and capital. The latter has all material things, all seen power, guns, ships, money and men. But with faith in the Father, the righteous have the most power, and they will ultimately wrench this earth from the grasp of the robbers. And then Father will deal with them, and we will have peace for once and forever. One of the most helpful books I ever owned was 'The Spirit of the New Testament,' written by a Boston woman. I picked it up in a second-hand book store in Denver. It gave me, in the beginning of my work, the clearest idea of Jesus' mission and the purpose of his life. It would do any one good to read it. But I have had to leave all earthly authority behind me and follow the Father. For every hour I am told, 'Follow me and I will do the rest.' Of myself I can do nothing, but with the Father all things are possible."

By the restlessness of our guest and his comments as to why he was so long detained in the Datils, he frequently saying that it all had a meaning, I knew the day was approaching when he would hear the summons, the order to move on whithersoever the Voice directed, to the place where the Spirit led.

"If you go south you will need money to cross the boundary. The guards won't let you pass free with that horse. They will detain, and may defeat you," I remarked.

"Have faith," he said, "I am doing Father's wish and will, and He knows the way I must go, and He is preparing it for me. No guard will stop me."

"But," I pleaded, "you are quiet and happy here. Your ministry of public healing has been completed for the present, and I am sure you will be safer here than in the mountains alone."

"When I came I told you that Father said I must go as soon as the people found out I was here. They have been talking it quietly for a long time, though no one knows it positively. But when they know I shall start."

His cool determination was apparent, and we had been expecting the announcement for days. The one thing now remaining was to exact a promise from him that he would write to let us know of his welfare. If he would only do that little courtesy it would take off the keen edge of uncertainty. The perilous, dangerous future would not be so oppressive if his friends could only know where he was, if still living. And, to break hours of silence, I asked:

"How will your friends know what has been your fate? How can they tell whether you are dead or not? You will surely die! What you have told me of your leading is enough to terrify the stoutest heart, for it's to be alone in some jungle or vast range, uninhabited except here and there a hut. You will die!"

"Have patience and faith," he quietly said. "Look within, and by the faith that's in you, you will know that I can not die. I was not born to die but to live — to do the Father's work. In His time He will bring me back. Suffer? Yes, but that is all. My hair will turn white, maybe in a night, but I can not die. I'll hear the roar of wild beasts and see the king of the forest, but nothing can harm me. If I am to do the work I must be protected, and I will be."

He ate little, talked less, slept more and lost interest in the topics he had so frequently discussed with vivacity. He gazed for hours into the fire. The face had lost its' cheer, the manner was tense, and answered in monosyllables. It was clear that he was listening to the Voice, much of the time, receiving instructions as to his future movements. He seemed startled sometimes, would silently spring to his feet and, with hands behind him, would pace for hours continuously and rapidly — which affected others unpleasantly. He changed perceptibly. He would arrange and rearrange his saddle. Mr. Swingle shod the horse and had brought extra sets of shoes from town. He had at first refused any gifts, but latterly took a slicker, leaving a coat in its place. He also accepted some trifles for Butte, and in rearranging them he would stand over the pack, thinking and looking; then commence and pace silently for hours. No one knew so well as he the horrible ordeal. To make it a little easier I gave him a gentle horse, one I thought he needed, and insisted on his accepting it.

"Please take Pet. You need an extra horse. Three hundred pounds is too much for Butte. Moreover, you say you are going to make forty miles a day. Butte can't make it. No horse can. If you make twenty, day in and day out, it will be a marvel."

"But Father will give Butte the strength the same as He does me. He has got to make more than twenty miles a day, Father says."

"Well," I replied, "I tell you, with three hundred pounds on him in a rough country, I can not see how he can survive such torture. If you go south, in some places it's well nigh impassable."

"Father will sustain him. He has got to make heavy journeys, long distances, for weeks to come," he replied, "particularly at first."

It was no use. Evidently his mind was made up, which would be the average way of expressing it. But, with him, I knew the Voice had said, "Go. Travel. All is in readiness." And we had proof of that later.

He finished his manuscript some days previous to his departure and said, with a sigh of relief:

"Take it. There it is. I, of myself, would never have written one word, but Father told me to write. They will now have ample time to make up their minds. I wouldn't have given them ten minutes; but He is kind. Take it to Denver and publish it. You are to publish it and manage it to suit yourself, for I shall be away along with the Father."

After a long, oppressive silence he spoke the only words that hurt. Very slowly, as though soliloquizing:

"But I, of myself, would never have trusted this to a woman. The responsibility is too great; the trust is too sacred. But Father says you are the right one, and He will open the door; that He will show you the way. Don't hurry, don't worry, don't struggle. In His time the door will open for you."

No words passed between us. The hour was set. I drove down to the postoffice Friday, March 27, and the first thing they handed me was a newspaper with the false telegram in it. I met Mr. Swingle and told him I felt sure the Healer might start at any hour, and if he was going too he had better be on hand.

When I got back, just before dark, our guest came out and stood silently looking at the rig, then at me. He seemed to be asking for news in every way but by words, and it was one of his striking characteristics that he had never once asked a single question about anybody or anything during the entire winter. Not once. It was a pardonable yielding to temptation that I kept the newspaper from him an hour or two. The children's letters he enjoyed always, commenting singularly once, when life to me seemed such a failure:

"Father says you have one thing the world can never take from you. It has tried in the past, and will in the future, but the world will fail."

Later, while he was looking at the burning, blazing resinous knots, I reached over and drew the paper from its hiding place and quietly handed it to him. He read it quickly, resenting its falsehoods, and sat listening to the Voice out of the Silence.

"Father says Sunday, day after tomorrow, I must go."

It made it none the easier because I had known it was coming. The silence was unbearable, and I bade him good-night.

Saturday Butte was not permitted to have any liberty. He was led back and forth to the spring, to the house for his noon lunch, and then to the barn, and securely tied in his stall. His lustrous eyes looked at his master inquiringly, and he droopingly stood waiting. No whinny for food or for fun. Even the horse felt the impending change, and I was afraid. The Healer read the Bible to me, and yet I felt that he was both anxious to leave and hesitating mentally. He wanted to go, was ready, and had been for ten days, but would rather not start if by any possibilitiy he could gain consent to remain a little longer.

"It is better not to mention it." he quietly said, as he pushed his chair from the table.

He went to the barn and was gone a long time. On entering the house he picked up his Bible and read for hours. When dinner was on the table and he was called he answered. "I can not eat."

All the afternoon he paced the house almost nervously. He was expecting and looking for Mr. Swingle, but at 4 o'clock I said, "I will speed the parting guest."

"What did you say?"

I then repeated it slowly. "Do you want your horse? If so, I will go myself and bring him here so you can saddle and pack him."

"Yes, go get him."

No horse ever crossed that canyon quicker. And by the time I was in front of the house the Healer had his saddle, blankets, sack, rod and all awaiting us. Mr. Swingle failed to put in an appearance. Butte was saddled, packed, and the Healer had mounted, when I found his canteen empty. "You won't need water, and it will be lighter on Butte," I suggested; but he replied, "We will go by the spring and fill it. I drink a great deal of water when I have no food."

So he rode there and I filled his canteen, but before I handed it to him and I asked in hesitancy:

"Ask Father if I can walk a little way and show you a dim old road where you won't be likely to meet any one."

"Father says you can go, but I will not meet any one."

We started over the hills and down a valley. I felt he was going to send me home, and presently he said:

"You have gone far enough. It will soon be dark."

"Here is your canteen of water." He slung the strap over his left shoulder, the heavy rod being suspended from the right.

I stood by Butte and took his hand in the long, perhaps the last, farewell; with bowed head, uncalled came the words:

"Please say the Lord's Prayer."

Afer a moment, in a tremulous whisper, I heard the Prayer that must have been engraved on the mighty mountain sides, on the blue vault of the sky, on interstellar space. Then he rode down the canyon alone. The white horse and rider had vanished from view.

> "It was a valley gentle as a dream;
> Cool, with three shadows, dewy, fragrant, sweet.
> The very stillness worshipped, and I heard
> The untold secret of the heart of prayer."

Edgar Lee Hewett, Director of the School of American Archaeology and the Museum of New Mexico. Photograph by F.E. Baker, Courtesy of the Museum of New Mexico, Negative Number 7326.

PART 3

THE COPPER ROD

Under a lone pine tree on the eastern slope of the Sierra Madre in Chihuahua, a few yards west of the Piedras Verdes river, there is an unmarked grave which, if known a generation ago, would have been a shrine to thousands.

In the spring of 1906, I was making an archaeological reconnaissance of this valley. My young guide said to me early one morning: "Years ago, when I was a little boy, I found a dead man under that big pine tree. I was going up the valley early in the morning to hunt our cows. I saw a man lying under the tree, covered with a gray blanket. I supposed he was asleep. In the afternoon as I came down, I saw he was still there, and went over to see him. He was dead. Very much frightened. I ran all the way down to the village and told the *jefe político*. They sent an inquest up, decided that the man had died of starvation and freezing. It was then dead of winter, and there had been a great blizzard in the south. So they buried the man there under the tree. He was a large man with long hair."

The boy's story interested me. Did the man have any possessions? Yes, he had a big white horse, hobbled on the hillside, and a fine western saddle. These were taken down to the plaza and used as community property. The children rode the horse about the hills until he died of old age. Some memories were stirring in my mind: large man, long hair, big white horse, large western saddle. My boy said he would take me to see the *jefe político* at the village if I wished. His story was confirmed in every detail by half a dozen eyewitnesses. Could I see anything that had been saved from the episode? Yes, the big saddle. It bore the trademark of a well known marker of saddles in Denver. Anything else? Yes, the saddle pockets. In one of them, a worn out Bible; on the fly leaf, the name, Francis Schlatter. Nothing more? Ah, yes! A long leathern holster.

It contained a *solid copper rod* the size and shape of a baseball bat.

My chain of evidence was complete. That night at my campfire, I resurrected as best I could from memory some ten-year-old notes.

In the summer of 1896, there was working at his cobbler's bench in Old Albuquerque a simple, modest Alsatian peasant. It became known that he had healing power. We heard of him fasting forty days in the desert beyond the Rio Grande. Then a Mr. Charles Fox, from North Denver, Colorado, whose family had with good reason come to have high regard for the healer, invited him to go to Denver as his guest and serve the many sick people who had heard of him. It was on this journey that I first saw and talked with Francis Schlatter — a powerfully built man, a typical European peasant in appearance and dress; finely shaped head with hair to the shoulders; not talkative, but not taciturn; quite communicative about himself.

I was then teaching in the Greeley College of Education, and during Schlatter's ministry at Mr. Fox's house I occasionally went down to watch the procedure. Schlatter appeared in the gateway of the front yard at exactly 6:00 A.M. daily, worked until 12:00, retired until 1:00, finished at 6:00 P.M. The waiting crowd, several blocks long, always passed in single file and in perfect order in front of him. Everyone was given a firm handshake (he used both hands), with an inaudible prayer, followed sometimes by, "Thank the Father, not me." I doubt if anyone received more than a half minute of time. The number treated daily reached thousands, the fame of the healer having reached to both coasts.

Schlatter took no pay, no credit, made no pretenions, as did the dozens of counterfeit Schlatters who followed and tried to imitate him. What he did was plainly above board. He was just a plain, honest peasant, doing something, as he believed, for suffering humanity. Hundreds testifed to the permanence of their cures. I have never tried to explain it; couldn't if I tried. I can only say it was the most astonishing thing of its kind that has ever come to my notice. There was only one mystery about him. He kept with him always, in a leathern holster, a *copper rod* of the size and shape of an ordinary baseball bat.

It was given out that Schlatter's mission in Denver would end in December. It did. The waiting list was still blocks long. He was seen east of Colorado Springs, riding south on a big white horse given him by Mr. Fox. He showed up at the home of Don Mariano Larragoite, at La Joya, New Mexico, on the Rio Grande near the mouth of Embudo canyon. He was a guest there for a few days; and a friend of mine, governess to Don Mariano's children, conversed with him frequently and gave me interesting facts concerning him.

He rode on to the south, avoiding the cities — Santa Fe, Albuquerque, Socorro — and became a guest for several weeks at the Morely ranch near Datil, New Mexico, Mrs. Morely being one of his devoted disciples. He was later seen riding south over the Mogollon Mountains in a heavy snowstorm. From there, Francis Schlatter disappears from mortal eyes. Endless was the speculation concerning his disappearance. It fell to me to find the answer, ten years later, on my chance camp on the eastern slope of the Sierra Madre in Mexico.

For sixteen years this story reposed in my little book of "horseback notes." In 1922 I found myself in the Piedras Verdes valley again, and again in the plaza of Nuevas Casas Grandes. Would I find any recollection of the Schlatter episode? Yes, plenty of it. At the *jefe político's* house I was recognized, and my interest in the incident recalled. Was there anything left of the possessions of the great healer? No, the saddle was worn out; not a leaf of the Bible to be found. But ah, *si! The copper rod!* Rather gingerly, it was brought in from the back room. My interest was restrained but obvious. On leaving, I asked those good people if there were any favor I could do for them. Yes. could I assist them in getting a school teacher from Chihuahua for their children for a few weeks in the fall? *Seguro.* I most eagerly contributed a modest check to their educational fund.

Again I rode away.

Some months later, a heavy express package was delivered to me at my home in Santa Fe. It was bundled in gunny sacks and tied with scraps of rope, the origin of the shipment carefully suppressed. Now, a museum man, accustomed to collecting unusual things from the ends of the earth, never grows indifferent to a new find. He never knows what may be coming out of an old bundle, but knows that it is likely to be something exciting. This one bowled me over. On cutting away the cords and strings and burlap, there emerged *the copper rod of the great healer, Francis Schlatter.*